BLIGHTY'S RAILWAYS

BLIGHTY'S RAILWAYS

By A. J. Mullay

AMBERLEY

Cover illustrations: J. & C. McCutcheon Collection.

First published 2014

Amberley Publishing
The Hill, Stroud
Gloucestershire, GL5 4EP

www.amberley-books.com

British Library Cataloguing in Publication Data.
A catalogue record for this book is available from the British Library.

ISBN 978 1 4456 3857 7 (print)
ISBN 978 1 4456 3874 4 (ebook)

Typeset in 10pt on 12pt Sabon.
Typesetting and Origination by Amberley Publishing.
Printed in the UK.

Contents

Introduction

Tracks were cleared. Scheduled services stopped. Only one train was allowed to proceed.

This happened on 14 August 1914, when a special train raced from London to Dover in eighty minutes. Its principal passenger was Sir John French, heading for the Continent, where he would command the new British Expeditionary Force. The South Eastern & Chatham Railway was pleased with this operational feat – achieved at nearly a mile a minute – believing that in bringing its usual operations to a halt and in facilitating the hastening of the commander to join his troops, their company had made a major contribution to the war effort at the start of the First World War.

Modern historians might see this differently. If 1914–18 witnessed some of the worst possible examples of military command, the actions, or lack of them, of Sir John French would stand high among them. In a recent book on the events of 1914, Sir Max Hastings refers to French as 'a poltroon', while the late Alan Clark, in his book *The Donkeys*, wrote of French's 'impaired capacity' and 'faltering approach'. The commander seemed unable to process or interpret military intelligence, showed indifference to his putative allies, and displayed personal behaviour bordering on the cowardly.

Yet the railway company had excelled itself, and would do so again and again, in meeting every challenge the armed services could make of it, and its employees would display great acts of courage in facing enemy action at sea and from the air. Not that the South Eastern was exceptional in all this. While it was later to receive a personal letter from Field Marshal Haig praising its supportive efforts, *all* British railways excelled themselves in the war, doing exactly what was required of them, and at some considerable costs to themselves.

It is tempting, looking back a century, to see the railways' efforts as representing their zenith as transport carriers, in inverse relationship to the near-disastrous conduct of the Army commanders at the time. Indeed, on the morning of 1 September 1914, the South Eastern had to lay on another special train, this time to hasten the Minister of War, Lord Kitchener, on his urgent errand to Paris to order Sir John French to stop retreating so far and so fast.

Meanwhile, Blighty's great railways would excel where the military would falter.

Before the Declaration

On 25 July 1914, the First Lord of the Admiralty, Winston Churchill, was playing with his children on the beach at Cromer. This was two days after Austria had issued an ultimatum to Serbia, but Churchill was not alone in refusing to believe that war was inevitable. He may not even have been aware that the Admiralty, which he represented in Cabinet, had already begun to take ships up from trade by this date, with railway-owned vessels very much to the fore.

British politicians had hitherto been principally concerned with the 'Irish Question', where a seemingly inevitable progress towards Home Rule was held up by the desire of the Unionists, then as now, to retain the closest possible links with Britain.

But it was from deep in the Continental land mass that a storm was coming which would change the United Kingdom, and Europe, forever.

To encircle the new state of Germany, a network of treaties had been set up offering protection to the smaller states, but putting the European powers on potential collision paths. And so it proved, when Austria demanded that Serbia allow it a free hand within the smaller nation to investigate the assassination of Archduke Franz Ferdinand. Serbia could not meet all of Austria's demands, and on 28 July 1914, the Austrians declared war, safe in the knowledge that their alliance with Berlin would deter Russia from moving to protect its Slavic neighbours. But Moscow hardly had a chance to do so as Germany almost immediately declared war on Russia.

The Schlieffen Plan now had to be put into effect. Its target was France; its purpose was a lightning victory; its instrument the railway …

* * *

Much historical controversy has surrounded the opening of the European war in 1914, with railway timetables demonised as the agent which pushed the Continent into conflict. In the 1960s, venerable historian A. J. P. Taylor published his theory that, so regimented were German rail timetables in 1914, it was impossible for the Kaiser's generals to reverse a decision to mobilise their army. It is true that the Schlieffen Plan dictated that Germany strike westwards initially to defeat the French, before turning to the east to destroy the slow-to-mobilise Russians. This required a fast knockout blow against France, as well as their allies the British (should they interfere), and Taylor, who described the plan as 'remorselessly academic', argued that railway scheduling generated a mechanised momentum which could not be stopped. Fellow historian John Keegan agrees that the German commitment to timetabling 'bordered on the neurotic'. Perhaps their commanders should have recalled the words of their Prussian predecessor Carl von Clausewitz, who once remarked that no battle plan ever survived contact with the enemy.

In London the declaration of war took on a baroque complexity. While British politicians appeared appalled at the progress of events in Europe, where the UK had a treaty obligation to protect Belgium – which assumed new significance – military chiefs and railway managers were not idle. On 31 July, the secretary of the Railway Executive Committee (REC) informed all the nation's railway companies that the Admiralty expected provisional plans for mobilisation to be activated. It is noticeable, however, that the secretary's letter was a copy of one sent by the Admiralty to the London & South Western Railway, and forwarded by that company to the REC's office. (In practice, Gilbert Szlumper was secretary of both the railway company and the REC.)

The Admiralty's ignoring of the committee, whether through ignorance of its existence or a preference for relying on existing liaison arrangements – the L&SWR, for example, operated Southampton Docks – will be examined later. After some indecision, Prime Minister Asquith finally demanded that German forces be removed from Belgium, with this ultimatum to expire at 2300 on 4 August. There was some confusion about the exact hour intended, and this was to cause traumatic problems for the Great Central Railway's ships, condemning dozens of men to a prison camp from the first hour of the war, as will be related.

In his history of Britain's railways in the First World War, historian Edwin Pratt relates how the companies were already preparing timetables of military traffic intensively in the two years before 1914. So intensively, indeed, that he records that one unnamed 'especially talented' timetable compiler worked himself into an early grave because of the 'strenuous and exhausting toil'. Certainly, the War Office paid some gratuities to rail managers who worked extra hours on the preparation of timetables, which presumably were designed to operate on the 'elapsed' principle, the original start point being 00.00. But it is difficult to envisage how detailed or exact these could be without taking into consideration contemporary conditions, or changes in equipment and staffing at some unspecified future date.

If there was no rigid timetable for politicians, there was at least a provisional arrangement for an armed response to any threat from a Continental enemy. Belated Army reforms carried out in the previous decade had created what we would now call a 'Fast Reaction Force' which could be shipped to wherever it was required. Called the British Expeditionary Force (BEF), it initially comprised six divisions, maintained at permanent readiness. It could be moved to an appropriate port for embarkation at short notice, the choice being dictated by whichever railway was the 'Secretary Company' to the relevant Army Command.

British politicians could declare war as and when they saw fit, secure in the knowledge that there was no immediate threat of invasion, thanks to the invincibility of the Royal Navy. But to describe the politicians as dithering would be to understate the case; the Cabinet was still undecided about sending the BEF to France at all, even as late as 6 August. On that date, ministers eventually decided that the Army could be sent to Amiens, but the military ignored this, according to Taylor, and ordered it to a destination already provisionally chosen: Maubeuge.

Prime Minister Herbert Asquith was profoundly unhappy about war, as well he might be – it would end his career, as he proved to be out of his depth in administering a government making unprecedented demands on its people. His Chancellor, David Lloyd George, was firmly anti-war, believing that diplomacy should be used to sort out international differences, but within a year he was to display a practical approach that would revolutionise the UK's industrial output and soon afterwards turn him into a war leader whom even Winston Churchill idolised.

* * *

In theory, liaison between railways and the military establishment should have been channelled through the Railway Executive Committee (REC), but the Government's formal letter, informing railway companies that they had been taken over, was sent out by a civil servant at the War Office. This missive was typed on stationery dated 4 or 5 August, quoting the Regulation of the Forces Act 1871 as the enabling legislation. This empowered the armed services to make use of the companies' 'plant', but the letter sent in 1914 was presumably from a standing 'draft' or what we would now call a template, and did not mention the existence of the REC, established formally just two years previously. (A press release issued later on 5 August did make up for this omission.) A subsidiary of the Board of Trade, with the latter's president as nominal chairman, the REC's central body initially consisted of the general managers of ten railway companies, with two more joining in 1916.

The committee's acting chairman was originally Sir Frank Ree of the L&NWR, recently succeeded by the L&SWR's Herbert Walker on the former's death in April 1914. A 'North Western' influence can be detected in the presence on the central committee of that company's 'allies', the Caledonian and Lancashire & Yorkshire, although it is probably a coincidence that Walker, now GM of the L&SWR, had previously been a 'North Western' employee for twenty-six years. It would have surely been more appropriate, or at least *as* appropriate, to include the London, Brighton & South Coast and Great Eastern, whose proximity to European ports was of paramount importance. Also, those companies liaising with the Army's Scottish and Irish commands should not have been omitted. Despite having had two years of peace in which to organise itself, the REC's entry into war was confused, to put it at its kindliest.

The committee's first circular to British railway companies stated that 'in view of the critical state of affairs existing at the present moment it is possible that the Government will take over all the Railways in Great Britain at short notice'.

However, correspondence, now in the NAS, between Walker and the secretary of the Railway Clearing House shows that the committee had no definite idea of how many railways it now controlled, and it certainly was not 100 per cent coverage anyway. The number communicated to the RCH was actually ten short of the real total, and a correcting letter had to be sent before the war was a month old.

Those intentionally omitted – as policy, not clerical error – included the busy underground systems of London and Glasgow, as well as a number of Welsh narrow-gauge lines, so traffic turnover was obviously not a factor determining the REC's involvement. Indeed, just to confirm how confusing the inclusion criteria were for narrow-gauge railways, the Ffestiniog, Leek & Manifold, and Southwold were 'controlled', while the Corris and Talyllyn were not. Such inconsistency towards Welsh railways handling slate – soon to be a much-needed commodity following bomb damage – shows once again that the authorities had no idea of what was ahead of them. What earned any railway automatic inclusion, irrespective of size or turnover, was the ownership of canals or ships.

Under Way

The first of 334 trains transporting the earliest units of the BEF reached the embarkation quay on Sunday 10 August at 08.15, thirty-three minutes early. Over one subsequent fourteen-hour period a train arrived at the Southampton quayside every twelve minutes – seventy-three of them in total, each being cleared and moved out empty in seven minutes. Only 150 feet separated ship and train, allowing immediate loading. The last of the first wave of BEF units reached Southampton at 18.00 on 10 August, twenty-two minutes early. Historian James Hamilton calculates that each train carried only 200 troops – a positively luxurious arrangement compared to later transport conditions. What is more surprising is how few of these soldiers were Regulars, a matter discussed in more detail later.

The L&SWR's Southampton Docks complex was the principal port of embarkation, the usual destination being Le Havre, and the Pratt volumes give the impression that the entire BEF made this crossing. In fact, the SE&CR vessel *Hythe* was to claim having landed the first British troops in France, and some units were taken to Boulogne and Rouen. For the record, the first to land at Le Havre were the 1st Bn Middlesex Regiment, followed by the 1st Cameronians. The first to arrive at Boulogne were the 2nd Argyll and Sutherland Highlanders, while the earliest at Rouen were the 2nd Royal Welch Fusiliers.

One of the five infantry divisions was kept in the UK by a government grown increasingly uneasy watching the relentless German march into Belgium – and this infantry reallocation in itself necessitated a logistically challenging transfer from Ireland to Great Britain – but the BEF had to be reinforced almost immediately. (And as early as December, the number of British casualties would exceed the size of the original BEF itself.)

The transfer of the Army across the Channel was carried out with a high standard of efficiency, which brought praise and gratitude from the senior commander, Sir John French, and the Minister for War, Lord Kitchener. German officers later admitted that they were surprised to meet British troops on the Continent so soon, believing that the BEF could not be transported until at

least a week later. With the REC not involved at this stage, the crucial factor in
ensuring such a successful operation lay in the link between the railway bringing
the trains to the dockside at Southampton – the London & South Western – and
the Army's Southern Command. While the movement of the BEF to embark
at Southampton may have appeared smooth to those commanders at the apex
of the military establishment, there were nevertheless victims in this hasty
scrambling of troops.

The 1st Bn Cameron Highlanders, for example, departed Glasgow in the
middle of the night of 9 August, in no fewer than four trains, including cattle
trucks for the battalion's horses. Unfortunately, these wagons had low headroom,
unsuitable for the kind of draught horse used by regimental transport units, and
at Southampton a 'great number' of these unfortunate animals were found to
have died on the marathon journey to the South Coast. In contrast, the 2nd
Bn Argyll and Sutherland Highlanders seem to have made a comparatively
smooth passage down almost the whole length of the UK from Fort George,
near Inverness, to Southampton, whence they crossed to Boulogne, as previously
mentioned. This was despite more problems with horses, which were hurriedly
requisitioned from local owners (who had received subsidies to purchase fodder
and make the animals available at short notice). It was difficult to deploy the
horses to pulling Army vehicles and into haulage teams for the short trip from
barracks to station. The idea that each battalion should have its own transport
was one which was later superseded, with a preferable centralising of logistical
resources, but in 1914 even infantry units were having to provide their own
'wagon trains', necessitating the inclusion of livestock wagons in troop train
formations.

Such journeys, from the north of England or Scotland, were partly being
undertaken at night, and could be fatally stressful. When Lieutenant John Reith
went to war with his rifle unit and its animals, he travelled part of the way in
the cattle wagons to try to calm the horses. One was dead before it reached
England, never mind France, and Reith ordered the carcass to be hauled out
on to the platform at Newcastle Central, much to the station staff's horror. The
recollections of veterans, like this author's grandfather, that 'it was the horses I
felt sorry for – even more than the men' come to mind.

Ships commandeered to carry troops out of Southampton were expected
to cross the Channel unescorted. The danger which submarines could present
was simply not understood at the time, and was learned about the hard way.
Within a matter of weeks a U-boat commanded by a captain with no combat
experience sank three cruisers in the Channel in a single night, with the Navy
initially believing that the losses were caused by mines. While the BEF crossed
unharmed, it was soon to be the turn of railway steamers to succumb, the first
to be mined being one of the GWR's Channel Islands ferries, at Scapa Flow in
the following January.

The Railways Commanded I

At this point it might be appropriate to outline which companies were providing rail services in Britain, at a time when they were, in most cases, at their most prosperous. Very few European nations had a 100 per cent privately owned rail network – along with Spain, Greece, and European Turkey, Britain's network was built with private capital, and run for profit. (Malta, Jersey, and the Isle of Man also ran completely commercial railway systems.) Of the UK's top thirty-four companies in terms of turnover, all thirty-four were making a profit in the year 1913. Cumulatively, their net income came to £52 million, after expenditure of £87.2 million had been subtracted from £139.25 million gross revenue. These figures proved seminal – they were taken by Government as a touchstone of financial performance even into the 1920s, when Britons and their railways had a very different relationship. The war would see an enormous increase in railway turnover, but an even bigger one in terms of outlay, leaving the net income virtually unchanged.

The other major protagonist nations in the war had at least an element of nationalisation in the way railways were constituted, not an insignificant fact when Britain's failure to increase line capacity for strategic purposes is considered. In Europe overall, approximately 116,000 of 216,000 miles were state-owned, some 55 per cent, as were more than two-thirds of Russia's lines in Europe. (And roughly the same proportion of Russian routes in Asia and Siberia.) France had a lower percentage of 'state' railways, slightly less than 20 per cent.

Britain's private enterprise railways were not likely to undertake the doubling of the mostly single Highland mainline in its entirety, and the state did not see itself as a railway builder. Edwin Pratt, a champion of private enterprise, conceded by 1914, that 'nothing whatever was done by the State to improve the land approaches to Scapa Flow' (the Orkney Islands base for Britain's Grand Fleet). This contrasted with the German construction of 'otherwise unnecessary sidings along the frontier with Belgium', and French financial assistance for the Russians to improve their rail links westwards. The latter undoubtedly contributed to the downfall of the Schlieffen Plan; with the Russians moving troops faster than the German High Command anticipated, it was forced to transfer divisions to the Eastern Front at a crucial time on the Western Front.

This was a positive result of governmental direction in railway building, something which was almost unknown in Great Britain. Indeed, a Government-appointed commission which had recommended a single Anglo-Scottish railway in the early 1840s was ignored by the business community, with three lines being completed by the end of the decade, whether the Government approved or not. Admittedly, the duplication of routes and stations, a direct result of competition between companies, was to prove beneficial to Britain in two world conflicts. In this newly declared war, the Government was effectively paying the companies a stipend on a regular retrospective basis through the offices of the REC – the first payment covered the five months to the end of 1914 – and this basically amounted to an undertaking that the companies' net profit in the year 1913 would be guaranteed every year while the railways were 'controlled'. Their gross and net income was public knowledge at the end of the war, as would be expected of limited companies. But such matters as passenger and goods carriage mileages were not available, even into the 1920s, and published annual reports contained redacted sections, where shareholders could not be given information about the company they had invested in. Obviously, a great deal of goodwill – patriotism perhaps – was required on the part of the Stock Exchange, but it places a question mark about whether it is desirable or practicable to place such a vital part of the war effort in commercial hands.

The REC's authority over the companies was established without detailed plans about how this would work out in practice, beyond the basic guarantee that the net profit of 1913 would be reproduced. But not all railway operations were predictable and there was a particular problem when some companies might be required to undertake comparatively trivial but frequently repeated tasks. Various contracting questions had to be at least examined, and it was arranged that accountants from six of the railways comprising the main REC would meet on 9 August to examine the matter. Even at that early stage, it had occurred to Government and the railways' owners that operational costs were not the only problem to be addressed. There were questions on depreciation and the loss of repair and rebuilding capacity. This would soon become pressing – the companies' works began undertaking manufacturing as the autumn drew on, to the detriment of their own rolling stock.

How this was resolved will be discussed later, and an assessment of the railways' financial performance in the First World War is made at the end of this book. What follows here is a brief pen-portrait of the principal companies.

* * *

Two railways competed for the title of 'Premier Line', and in describing the Great Western ahead of the London & North Western, it is primarily because the latter was already beginning to work closely with another company, the Lancashire & Yorkshire, with which it would merge (effectively, take over) in 1922. Such a trend would continue, with the takeover of the Hull & Barnsley by the North Eastern, and there would doubtless have been others if the 1923 'Grouping' had not taken place. In that year nearly all 150 rail companies in Britain were grouped into four consortia, very much as a result of the war which began in 1914.

The company nearest to the Front Line geographically was the South Eastern & Chatham. The product of an amalgamation in 1899 between two rival lines, this company served the ports of Folkestone, where it owned the harbour, and

Dover, as well as resorts on the Kent coast. Its London termini were at Charing Cross and Cannon Street, with a share of platforms at Victoria. From a martial point of view, it served the Woolwich Arsenal and Dockyard, as well as the naval base of Chatham. Being so placed, one might have expected the South Eastern to have moved the BEF to one of the Channel ports. The British Government's intention was always to strengthen the resistance of France to a Continental enemy pushing west and south through Alsace and Lorraine before heading directly southwards for Paris. The hostile invasion of the Low Countries was never anticipated – curiously, in view of the need of such countries as the UK to guarantee the safety of Belgium by the 1839 Treaty of London. The army intended to support France was planned to land at Le Havre following a cross-Channel passage from Southampton. This made sense in that the latter port had a proper docks system which would facilitate the embarkation of an entire army – although the British Expeditionary Force (BEF) was barely that.

In addition, the South Eastern's loading gauge (a profile which dictated the dimensions of loads carried, or vehicles accepted from other networks) was lower than that of the London & South Western, so the latter had the task of moving what most British people probably believed was 'the Army' that would deal with the Germans. In peacetime, the South Eastern had offered a journey of less than seven hours' duration from London to Paris – faster than travelling to the capital of Scotland. In war, the port of Folkestone became a prime point of contact with the Army in France, prompting the Government to take it over altogether before the close of 1915.

Increasing its difficulties, the South Eastern had to deal with undiminished demand for day trips to the seaside, at the same time as organising military traffic. This resulted from the newly activated REC giving a green light to the companies to continue holiday traffic as war broke out in the first week of August, and even permitting holiday excursion traffic to continue to the end of November 1914. In addition to all this, the company's ships made a major contribution to the war at sea, as will be related in the relevant chapter. That an SE&CR steamer took its place among the armoured warships at Jutland hardly seems believable.

Westwards along the South Coast was located the London, Brighton & South Coast Railway, which shared Victoria with the South Eastern. Its principal passenger traffic may have been with Brighton, but the port of Newhaven provided a link with Dieppe, and the company advertised this as 'The Royal Mail Route'. Although known as a passenger line, it was this company which was involved in a collision between three goods trains in 1918, all three of them carrying ammunition. Fortunately, there were no casualties, the 'Brighton' finding that its generous loading gauge – the most accommodating south of the Thames, and some 5 inches higher than the SE&CR – made it a very suitable freight conduit.

West of here was the domain of the London & South Western, a company which described itself, with some reason, as 'England's military line'. By the end of the war it connected with no fewer than 176 military camps, in a network including such strategic centres as Salisbury Plain and Southampton, as well as the capital. But its introduction to war was confused. Having just undertaken the movement of the 1st London Division to Wareham and Wool in Dorset on 28 July, apparently on exercise, with ten trains already at their destination and a further eight on the way, the company discovered that events on the Continent had caused the authorities in London to have a panicky rethink. The eight trains were turned around on route, and the troops ordered to re-embark on the first ten (despite their Dorset destination being comparatively convenient for Southampton). On 3 August, and in advance of the British ultimatum, the South Western then moved the Home Counties (Territorial) Brigade from Salisbury Plain to depots and barracks nearer London: no fewer than 14,000 troops, seventy-eight guns, and 1,387 horses were moved through the wayside station of Amesbury on that date.

Transport historian Edwin Platt suggests that these movements showed the railway company at its most efficient, which is undeniable, but with neither division being moved nearer Southampton, there is some evidence of confusion in the orders received from Southern Command, for which the L&SWR held 'secretary' status. Like the London & North Western, and the Great Western, the company had already set up a military department to concentrate on troop transport arrangements when these became necessary. Incidentally, when preparing paths for individual troop trains approaching Southampton, the South Western prepared its timetables backwards from the arrival time, detailing where and when each linking company would pass on the crowded trains.

Unlike its 'North Western' rival, the Great Western led a comparatively untroubled existence from the days when Isambard Kingdom Brunel was laying broad-gauge tracks westwards from London's Paddington to connect with Birmingham, South Wales, Bristol, and the farthest parts of the West Country. The company even emerged unscathed from the 1923 Grouping as one of the four consortia, and only lost its identity with Nationalisation in 1948 – although it still had its admirers even then. A change of gauge was completed in 1892 when GWR tracks were standardised with all other British companies, although it was arguable that a broader gauge had economic advantages in terms of permitting higher loads per vehicle, and greater stability at high speed. Brunel's experimentation with atmospheric propulsion was probably ahead of its time, but his reputation as an engineer was already assured, and the products of the company's works at Swindon created a tradition of Great Western grandeur in the form of handsome locomotives in Brunswick Green with copper-capped chimneys. Passenger stock livery was settled as 'chocolate and cream' and there was a thriving coal traffic based on the output of the South Wales collieries.

The most northerly point on the GWR network was Warrington, reached on a joint line which will feature in this war story. The company's ships were active in two world wars, and their work in the first conflict will be discussed in the appropriate chapter.

The London & North Western Railway faced its London public with a magnificent Doric arch at Euston, one which survived until the iconoclastic 1960s arrived. The company reached as far north as Carlisle, also serving the Lancashire cities, as well as Leeds and Birmingham. The 'Irish Mail' was the nation's oldest named train service, operating to Holyhead, whence Ireland was reached by North Western steamers. This mercantile activity was an important part of the company's work, and by 1910 steamer services were being co-ordinated with, and advertised alongside, those of the Lancashire & Yorkshire. Crewe was not only the most famous junction in Britain, but also the company works, where everything from rails to locomotives was manufactured for the company's own use – and in 1914–19 also for the Government's. Having mentioned the 'Lancs & Yorks', it's appropriate to discuss them next, particularly as the Grouping was to see the latter company's CME at Horwich apparently rank ahead of the North Western's at Crewe.

The name of the Lancashire & Yorkshire accurately indicated the geographical area covered by the company. It reached the sea at Fleetwood on the west coast and Goole on the east, with extensive maritime activity taking place under the company flag. The L&Y's closeness to the L&NWR, particularly in marine matters, would lead to the company being included on the original REC, and a merger with the Euston-based concern in 1922. Unlike another 'middle England' company, the Great Central, the Lancs & Yorks never succeeded in building a connection to London.

With Derby at its heart, the Midland was a prosperous company, whose locomotive livery of Crimson Lake was arguably the most handsome of all the pre-Grouping concerns, and was adopted by its successor, the London, Midland & Scottish. Even some Stanier Pacifics carried Midland colours well into the 1960s. The transport of coal was the company's staple traffic, necessitating the early introduction of Control measures, but the Midland could boast express services running the length of England from St Pancras more than 400 miles to Carlisle, where it greeted two allied companies offering services throughout most of Scotland. The Midland was, perhaps surprisingly, the largest single investor in the Forth Bridge Railway. All this was made possible by the construction of the Settle & Carlisle route, probably the finest main line built over difficult terrain in the entire UK. In 1912, the Midland had taken over the London, Tilbury & Southend, and as a result had the dubious honour of being the first railway in Britain to be bombed from the air.

The Great Central might have been regarded as another Middle England railway, rather like the Lancashire & Yorkshire in having a strong industrial base and access to ports on both east and west coasts. Unlike the L&Y, the GCR transformed itself from its original existence as the Manchester, Sheffield & Lincolnshire by forging a main line south to London, the last built into the capital, and terminating at Marylebone. The company's GM, Sir Sam Fay, was 'recruited' by the Ministry of War in 1916, and was involved in military manpower planning at the highest level.

The Great Eastern served Essex and East Anglia, with an important ferry terminal at Harwich. The war would make considerable demands on the company – not only in running its train services, but in operating North Sea routes while under attack from submarines and destroyers, and then having to undergo raids from the air. Logic suggests that the GER should have taken over the London, Tibury & Southend in 1912, but lost out to the Midland.

Three companies made up the East Coast Main Line (ECML), a major artery stretching 520 miles from London (King's Cross) to Aberdeen. The companies were the Great Northern, North Eastern, and North British, and their part in operating this route – which could have been targeted by enemy aircraft – is discussed later. Suffice to say that the Great Northern stretched from London into Lincolnshire and Yorkshire, with its engineering works at Doncaster, soon to become an important part of the military machine. In 1914 the company had few military associations, but the next five years saw the establishment of two major camps at Grantham, one for machine-gun training, and also what became the RAF's principal training college, at Cranwell, near Sleaford.

The North Eastern enjoyed a monopoly in its area of England, between the Tweed and Doncaster, with branches into Westmoreland and running-powers not only to Edinburgh, but over the Forth Bridge, in which it had a major shareholding. The company suffered a painful introduction to modern warfare when German surface ships bombarded three East Coast towns in December 1914. Worst affected were the Hartlepools and their experience is described later in this book. Three railwaymen were killed, the first of more than thirty who died working on Britain's railways in a country unaccustomed to the threat of destruction or invasion. The company owned docks here and, extensively, at Hull, making it the largest dock-owning railway in the country. Its policy towards shipping was to invest in commercial lines, such as Wilson's. Its Deputy GM, Eric Geddes, became a major figure in the upper reaches of both the Army and the Admiralty, as well as the first-ever Minister of Transport.

The North British was the largest Scottish company, if not the most prosperous, despite handling cross-Border traffic on two main lines and enjoying a monopoly of the Fife coalfield. By reason of proximity to Edinburgh Castle, it was appointed as liaison company to Scottish Command and serviced Rosyth naval base, the home of Beatty's scouting forces in the first half of the war, and then latterly the Grand Fleet. The Caledonian styled itself as the national railway for Scotland, serving as the northern end of the WCML while also providing access to Perth and Aberdeen. Its blue locomotive livery was so distinctive as to be considered by the BTC for express power nationally in 1948, by which time the 'Caley' had been part of the LMSR for a quarter of a century. It enjoyed links with the L&NWR which ensured it the only Scottish place on the REC.

There were three other Scottish companies, the most important of which, for this historical survey, was the Highland. This principally comprised a single line north from Stanley Junction, just north of Perth, to Inverness, and then on via Invergordon to the Far North coast, locations soon to be crucial in Britain's naval defence. There was also a lengthy branch to the west coast at Kyle of Lochalsh, another strategically important area.

Irish railways were not affected by the activation of the REC in 1912, which again failed to mesh with the relevant Army Command Centre. However, as early as the autumn of 1914, the committee included Irish companies in its dissemination of military equipment orders. An Irish committee was formed in 1916, the year when the independence movement in the south of the island reached a new level. The two largest companies were the broad-gauge concerns, the Great Northern and Great Southern & Western, the former responsible for the main trunk route between Dublin and Belfast, although the latter had a larger network, with the Dublin–Cork route as its centrepiece. Unlike Great Britain, Ireland hosted a large number of narrow-gauge lines, some quite extensive, like the County Donegal (125 miles).

* * *

There was some inconsistency in the make-up of the ten-strong managing committee of the REC in 1914, including the Great Northern, which owned no ships and served no major military bases at that time, but omitting the Great Eastern, LB&SC, and North British, all three of which qualified on both counts. Two of these were later absorbed on to the board, although not the NBR, leaving the Caledonian as the only Scottish representative. Making the Edinburgh company's omission all the more curious was its role as Secretary Company to Scottish (Army) Command; within two years the North British would also be tasked with passing air-raid warnings to other Scottish railways, a function undertaken by the REC itself south of the Border. Meanwhile, the Army's Irish Command liaised with the Great Northern of Ireland, a company similarly excluded from the Committee's organising body, and it would be 1916 before a decision was made to establish an Irish REC. In effect, this arrangement in the overall UK failed to mesh completely with the Army's new command structure, finalised in January 1911, omitting two out of six liaison companies.

Railway Company Liaison with Army Command Centres, October 1914–16

Army Command	Location	'Secretary' Company	REC membership*
Northern	York	North Eastern	Yes
Eastern	London	South Eastern & Chatham	Yes
Southern	Tidworth	London & South Western	Yes
Western	Chester	London & North Western	Yes
Scottish	Edinburgh	North British	No
Irish	Dublin	Great Northern of Ireland	No

*of the REC's governing body consisting of railway General Managers

Having met only six times before the end of July 1914, and despite its failure to fully recognise the Army's command structure, the new committee stepped up its activities to a frenetic level. Based at the L&NWR's Westminster offices in Parliament Street, it was in an almost continuous state of convocation in the first three weeks of August, with daily meetings scheduled for 10.00, 14.00, 18.00, and 21.15, with, in addition, staff being told to be contactable at any other time. Staff in August 1914 numbered no more than six, with seventeen being the maximum at any one time in later years. By 24 August 1914, the frequency of meetings had settled down at twice daily, slowing to three times weekly from the 29 August. This regime lasted until the following January, when meetings of the full committee began to be held weekly, but with 'special' meetings held when necessary. One railway whose GM was unable to attend initially was the Lancashire & Yorkshire, whose representative had been holidaying in Germany, although he was allowed to return by 21 September.

Unfortunately, the REC got off to bad start with one of its first communications. On 16 September 1914, the Executive's acting chairman circulated all railways, expressing concern that the outbreak of war had happened at such a time, early August, that many citizens 'were not able to get away for their summer holidays'. As a result, Walker sanctioned the companies to extend excursion fare offers beyond 30 September. The Great Northern, in whose archival files this copy letter was found, immediately announced that a new cut-off date of 30 November would be introduced, so as to allow visitors time and opportunity to travel to 'seaside towns and holiday resorts', although not including Scottish or Irish destinations. This casual attitude misfired horribly in succeeding years, resulting in rail companies having to operate normal passenger services at the height of summer, while facing unprecedented demands for coaching stock for troop movements, and all this with a suddenly diminishing labour force.

In practice, it appears that the REC's pronouncement merely confirmed that normal service could continue uninterrupted. Posters conveying stern warnings were understood, by staff and passengers alike, to be purely precautionary (and, curiously, the posters concerned were produced by the Railway Clearing House, not the committee established by the Board of Trade specifically to address liaison between railway companies and the military command). As the war went on, the REC's policy announcement of September 1914 encouraged civilians to *expect* continuing holiday arrangements at a time when huge demands were being made on the network in the form of troop specials and entirely new freight traffic streams.

Perhaps this preoccupation with holidays was not entirely a British characteristic. When units of the BEF took up positions around Mons on 23 August, they were astonished to see local people, whom they had assumed were escaping refugees, crowding on to an excursion train bound for the seaside!

* * *

But the REC's relationship with the Royal Navy at this time was even worse, or was arguably non-existent. When writing to all the companies on 22 July, the Admiralty appeared to ignore the committee altogether, their Lordships' letter headed succinctly 'Navy War Order System'. The 'system' consisted of companies being expected to volunteer their ships for naval service at short notice on the 'you, you, and you' principle. Astonishingly, on the day the letters were being opened in the railways' head offices, 23 July, Lloyd George, Chancellor of the Exchequer, told the House of Commons that relations with Germany were 'very much better than they had been'. Later in the day, however, came the news of the Austrian ultimatum to Serbia, the former nation being linked to Germany by treaty in the event of war. What happened in Britain over the next fortnight suggests that the military, and transport managers, had a greater understanding than politicians of how the linked treaties would cause an unstoppable 'domino effect', and what practical arrangements for war would have to be made by military personnel and civilians alike.

The aforementioned Regulation of the Forces Act 1871 empowered the armed services to make use of Britain's railways at a time of war, and in the case of the companies' ships, it was made clear that, although compensation would be paid, the company might not want its vessels back again. (A more detailed discussion of railway ships at war is recounted in a separate chapter.)

Manpower (and Horsepower)

Before the war, many railwaymen had joined the territorials, spending much of their limited leisure time drilling in halls at weekends. This took on special significance for the railways as soon as war was declared – the North Eastern, for example, immediately lost 2,000 men to the colours in the first month, just as the troop trains started rolling. In addition, many of the company's remaining staff formed a Territorial battalion (the 17th, a Service Battalion of the Northumberland Fusiliers, a regiment embroiled in the Continental war from the first day at Mons). These railwaymen soon found themselves building and repairing light railways at the Front, even under fire.

Incidentally, military historians have wondered how the Army expected to win a war while reservists made up the bulk of the infantry. While the railways now had too few experienced railwaymen, the infantry battalions had too many. Historians Krijnen and Langley (see Bibliography under Richards) have made the point that the *majority* of soldiers now entraining in the BEF in August 1914 were 'weekend' men. The average infantry battalion consisted of around 990 ORs (Other Ranks), and in the case of the Northumberlands, 640 of them were reservists. Even worse were the King's Own Scottish Borderers with 700 and, worst of all, the Royal Fusiliers with 735. When war was declared, regular soldiers had tended to be dispersed in barrack and sentry duties, while reservists would report *en masse* in answer to a telegram appeal (or order) and would immediately be entrained.

From the first week of war, the railway companies were having to undertake holiday seasonal traffic, in addition to military specials, while operating with reduced staff complements. They were 'reduced' by as much as 34 per cent in some cases, for one of the biggest contributions made by the railways was in manpower, and the call-up of territorials was just the beginning.

No fewer than 184,000 men left railway employment to join the armed services in the fifty-one months of war. This was enough to crew the Grand Fleet three times over, or the equivalent of eighteen Army divisions – in comparison, the original British Expeditionary Force comprised only six. Additionally, some 2,000 senior staff left railway employment 'on loan' to Civil Service departments.

* * *

At the time of the declaration of war, the railways of Britain had employed 625,559 workers, of whom 284,334 were operational staff. Obviously, to lose 184,000 men over the next four years represented an enormous proportional loss, while contributing in no small manner to the nation's fighting performance. But these numbers challenged the remaining managers and staff with unexpected, indeed unreasonable, operating problems.

This enthusiasm for enlistment seems to have taken the railway companies, and the REC, by surprise, although perhaps enthusiasm was only part of the problem. In August 1914 the Army was paying recruiting sergeants a bonus of half a crown (12.5p) for every new recruit, the equivalent of £10 nowadays. With men queuing to enlist, this must have been a lucrative time for some fortunate NCOs, and the bonus was reduced to 1 shilling by November of that first year. Doctors at recruiting offices were also on a bounty for new recruits and before long were ordered not to process more than eight per hour.

In the first week of September, with the war barely a month old, the Committee's Acting Chairman sent out REC Circular 61, containing the following:

> Some action should be taken to prevent so many men leaving the railway service as would render it difficult to find means to carry out, not only the requirements of the public, but also the requirements of the Army and Navy authorities in case of emergency. It is obviously not the wish of any of us to discourage men to enlist, but at the same time, it is felt that a man … is rendering as good service to the State by remaining at his employment as he could possibly be if he enlisted with the Forces.

The Circular added that the War Office had now been asked that recruiting officers should insist that a railwayman seeking to enlist must produce a release document from his present employers. If he had gone so far as to leave the railway in order to join the colours, he should be considered to have resigned and 'no special steps should be taken to hold his position open for him on his return from the War'.

* * *

By the end of the war, the L&NWR and North Eastern had lost just over one third of their workforce to the Services. The Great Western had lost just under one third, and Great Central and Great Northern each 30 per cent. Casualty rates among the enlisted varied among these companies from around a fairly typical 11 per cent to a horrendous 36 per cent in the case of the Great Central and just on 30 per cent among ex-railwaymen from the Midland. Why there should be such a discrepancy among the casualty figures is not obvious, but a fuller analysis is attempted in the final part of this volume.

One railway lost its entire staff to the Services – the Avonmouth Light Railway – both of whose staff members enlisted. But this 100 per cent figure was surpassed by the Metropolitan District (comprising the Central London, City & South London, and London Electric railways), which started with 2,499 staff, of whom 2,732 enlisted. There was obviously a regular turnover in staffing these companies, many of whose jobs could be undertaken by women, and the neighbouring Metropolitan Railway – which was advertising 'Supper Trains' and Golf Specials well into 1915 – also had a seriously high enlistment rate.

Curiously, after the war, the Bishop of Peterborough preached a eulogy to those railwaymen who had left the nation's primary transport network for others to run, and, in some cases early in the war, were allowed to do so by their employers in direct conflict with the REC's instructions. The Great Eastern Railway even established an assessment centre for the military recruitment of its staff at Liverpool Street. Unfortunately, the railway coach housing the centre would be bombed from the air, with some loss of life. Railway staff need not go to war; it would come to them.

* * *

Nowadays we can only look back with horror at the ordeal of trench warfare in the First World War, so it seems scarcely believable that there was such enthusiasm among young men to become involved. And it is a comment on the unpleasant, poorly-paid, and uncongenial nature of manual work on the nation's rail network that there was such an overwhelming response to Kitchener's appeal for volunteers in 1914. But did Lieutenant Siegfried Sassoon's batman at the Somme *have* to be a GWR signalman?

An individual case history can give us an inkling of what faced a young railwayman joining His Majesty's forces in 1914. Norman McKillop was a youth employed as an engine cleaner on the North British for twopence (1.5p) an hour. Norman enlisted as soon as he had seen Lord Kitchener's 'Your Country Needs You' poster and soon found himself, lacking any proper military training, retreating with an infantry battalion on Belgian soil. His family then received a telegram announcing that Norman had been 'killed by a mule' – fortunately a misprint for 'kicked by a mule', and after hospitalisation, he was on his way to Mesopotamia and then East Africa. His memoirs give the impression that this was all a bit of a lark before getting down to the serious peacetime business of driving Gresley Pacifics and writing about his footplate experiences under the pseudonym 'Toram Beg'. His was a tough generation.

* * *

It could have been predicted that Kitchener's call for volunteers would find an immediate response in the coalfields, where conditions could be equally described as highly uncongenial, and even more dangerous than on the railways. It was, after all, less than a year since the Senghenydd Colliery disaster, which claimed 440 lives in a single incident, with owner and manager receiving paltry fines. No fewer than a quarter of a million miners enlisted in the first thirteen months of war, at the end of which time a shortfall had appeared in the coal production figures to the tune of nearly thirty million tons. Did it not occur to military recruiters that signing up colliery men, dockers, and railway staff might create a problem less than a year into the war?

Perhaps the only job worse than working on the railways, or coal mining, matching either for unpleasant conditions, poor pay, and, not least, mortal danger, was stevedoring. This was conducted on what was basically a daily contract, with hiring taking place competitively each morning at the dock gates. At least miners and railway staff were actually *employed*, although it must have seemed little in the way of a blessing. Perhaps not surprisingly, when the Government discovered in 1916 that it would have to address labour shortages in logistics, it was stevedoring which was the most pressing. The Transport Battalions formed early in that year were put to work in the docks, where there had been no question of employment security (in more than one sense), but within the year, the battalions were also being allocated to work on canal wharves and railway goods sheds. This reflected the Government's casual 'take em all' attitude to recruiting, even from such vital occupations as transport operation.

Making matters worse, in March 1915 railways were banned from offering employment to a man of military age unless he had already been excused service. As a result the companies were forced to seek labour from those under the age of eighteen, thus lowering the standards of skills and experience available among their staff complements. Strength too was diluted, companies finding what Edwin Pratt calls 'a loss of physical capacity' in station staff. There proved to be insufficient men, or insufficiently strong men, to load or unload troop supplies quickly, and Pratt refers to contractors having to be brought in. Who they were and how they were able to employ suitable workers was not revealed, and this was the problem the Transport Battalions were later formed to tackle. In many cases women could be recruited in large numbers, but the existing staff structure suffered, with the question of seniority becoming contentious. Soon it was not unusual for footplate crews to comprise two drivers, one of whom might be only slightly junior to the other, but was expected to undertake firing. Happily, many such cases were resolved by the drivers themselves splitting their duties half and half.

* * *

Another 'recruiting' problem concerned horses, a matter addressed in REC Circular 4, within twenty-four hours of the declaration of war. As mentioned earlier, the Army had an arrangement with horse owners in the vicinity of a regimental barracks or depot that a subsidy would be paid for fodder, in return for the horse being made immediately available to the military in the event of an emergency. With every unit, including infantry, requiring horses for the transport of their own equipment or supplies – the troops themselves were expected to march from the railhead to the Front – draught animals became as valued as racehorses. The REC soon received reports of the Army requisitioning animals belonging to the railways; obviously, horses used for shunting wagons in goods depots would be ideal for military transport. The Great Western, for example, supplied 273 horses to the military, of which only 221 were definitely paid for. As early as 5 August, twenty-four hours into the First World War, the railways were being given the name of a War Office contact, Lt-Col. McMunn DSO, to whom they could communicate their concerns. One suspects that this would be futile; it was near impossible to bring back companies' valued employees once enlisted, never mind their animals.

* * *

As if to confirm how railway pay failed to match that of other technical careers, the South Eastern and Chatham management was soon dismayed to find that staff were resigning in numbers to take up better-paid work at Woolwich Arsenal. Not surprising, perhaps, when the figures are examined. REC acting chairman Sir Herbert Walker commented at the end of the war that the 'average railwayman' had been paid 27 shillings a week in 1914, but by 1921 this had been supplemented by an additional 46 shillings. But munitions work was soon paying more than £10 weekly – for men and women.

Railway staff were divided into three categories – 'railwaymen', footplate staff, and clerks – represented by two trade unions, the National Union of Railwaymen (NUR) and Associated Society of Locomotive Engineers and Firemen (ASLEF). The Railway Clerks Association, although formed in 1897, was not recognised by Government until February 1919. As it was, the two unions had negotiated together with a committee of General Managers for a 'war bonus' at the beginning of 1915, and from 13 February of that year a supplement of 3 shillings a week (15p) was paid to those earning less than 30 shillings (£1.50), and 2 shillings over that figure. It had been agreed among the managers – effectively the REC's managing committee in all but name – that one-quarter of the increase would be borne by the companies, the rest by Government. The REC did not become formally involved until 1917, but there were further bonuses declared twice before the end of 1915, one in the following year, two in the year after that, and one in 1918. Even then, there was a partial strike in the last year of the war.

Staff–employer relationships gave every appearance of unions pursuing management, who gave ground like a retreating army, no doubt conscious that their workers were an irreplaceable asset – almost literally irreplaceable since the imposition of Government-imposed recruitment restrictions early in 1915. While staff pay was becoming more realistic at a time of increasing food prices – a jump of 176 per cent between 1914 and 1920 - there was still no limit on working extra hours, whenever required. Additionally, railway work had become even more dangerous than before, with railways becoming a favourite target for German aerial bombing, with work often having to be carried out in blackout conditions.

Female staff were not included in pay discussions and were clearly regarded as temporary, although most railways had employed women even before 1914. There was a partial application of the War Bonus to women workers, as from 19 December 1916: an additional 3 shillings (15p) weekly to women aged over eighteen, and 1s 6d (7.5p) to those under that age. But 'partial' is the operative word, with ten companies mean-spiritedly declining to offer it – the Great Northern, North Eastern, SE&CR, two companies in Wales, and all of them in Scotland.

* * *

In addition to seeing their operating staff 'escaping' to the forces, railway management soon found that many of their employees were working directly, and exclusively, for the military. Lloyd George was to write in his *War Memoirs* that, so challenging were transport problems on the Western Front, 'disaster was narrowly averted by the aid of a civilian expert' – this was the North Eastern's Eric Geddes. At that time the Army was in the process of lengthening its share of the Front Line. In September 1914 this was a mere 20 miles; its length would fluctuate depending on martial conditions, but it would be six times as long by 1918. Geddes rose through the upper echelons of, firstly, the Army, then the Royal Navy, where he ended up as First Lord of the Admiralty, the post held by Winston Churchill at the outbreak of war. While commanding the Navy, Geddes introduced one of his former assistants from the NER, George Beharrell, who provided statistical evidence that the convoying of merchant ships reduced the number torpedoed – it seems tragic that this was not perfectly obvious to their Lordships, and doubly so that it had to be proved through statistics.

The Midland's Guy Granet followed Geddes into Army service, rapidly gaining contacts and prestige which would later make him the moving force behind the London, Midland & Scottish Railway after 1923, while Sir Vincent Raven, designer of the North Eastern's elegant Atlantic locomotives, was directed to a senior administrative post at the Woolwich Arsenal. A railway official who became President of the Board of Trade, no less, was Sir Albert Stanley, formerly Managing Director of the Underground Electric Railway in London, who was found a Parliamentary constituency in 1916 so that he could take on the Trade post. This was only one aspect of Stanley's remarkable career – in 1947, as Lord Ashfield, he would be invited to become one of only five full-time members of the then-new British Transport Commission.

Another railwayman joining Government was the General Manager of the Great Central, Sir Sam Fay, who was asked to join the Ministry of War in January 1916 but declined to wear a uniform in his appointment as the somewhat peculiarly named 'Director General of Movements'. He did however indulge himself by keeping a GCR locomotive standing by with steam up at Gerrard's Cross, the station nearest to his home, at times when he might be required to make an urgent journey to London.

It was perhaps just as well that senior railway management found themselves welcomed into the upper realms of military and logistical administration.

Having railways' GMs or chairmen within the Whitehall establishment must have softened the blunt nature of demands made on the railways. As it was, the Railway Executive Committee was conducted as a messenger service conveying military requirements to the railway companies without apparent assessment as to how appropriate, or practical, these might be. New working arrangements from 2 January 1917 were admonitory in tone, applying to a civilian service which had already assured Field Marshal Haig of the supply of all the equipment demands he could make. (Haig at least tried to acquaint REC representatives with the reason for his 'requests', with his grotesque invitation to visit the Somme battlefield.)

Approximately half of the Circulars – also known as 'Instructions' – are simply orders issued on behalf of the military establishment, interspersed with what are basically advice notes on how to work within the latest Army or Navy strictures, or asking for information on how individual companies were handling the latest military demands. To be fair to Sir Herbert Walker, he was personally prepared to argue that the railways were doing quite enough already. His interview with Kitchener in March 1915 on manpower demands was a case in point. Nevertheless, the file of 'Instructions' to the railways – commercial organisations – is ample evidence of how the companies and their workforces selflessly dedicated themselves to victory.

Orders Are Orders

Works, Rolling Stock

The Royal Navy was not only active in ship requisition before and immediately after the declaration of war, while the politicians wrung their hands. On 1 August, the South Eastern & Chatham was ordered to supply – in forty-eight hours, no more – two ambulance trains to work to and from Chatham Naval Hospital. Each rake would comprise eleven specially adapted vehicles, although corridor or 'vestibule' connections were not specified, and the trains, which the company provided so promptly and patriotically, were returned to South Eastern by the end of the year. Perhaps a little ungratefully, the Admiralty now turned to the London & North Western on the 6th, requesting another such train to be assembled and delivered at Chatham 'urgently'. Wolverton C&W works obliged after continuous work over a thirty-hour period, and Naval Ambulance Train No. 1 arrived at the base at four o'clock in the morning of the 8th. Naval orders for four more such trains followed shortly after. Making this all the more remarkable was the fact the L&NWR was already assembling three ambulance trains at Wolverton for the War Office.

Complicating matters were the differing design requirements of Army and Navy. The former preferred fixed cots, similar to bunks, while naval wounded would be conveyed in hanging cots (in fact hammocks, basically). It could be argued that keeping a casualty continuously in his own cot facilitated his move from ship to road vehicle to train, and would probably minimise pain and suffering during transfer. And it is a telling comment on the physical stature of sailors a century ago that their sickbeds needed to be no more than 70 inches in length. All but one of the naval trains conveying these casualties comprised twelve corridor vehicles, with most of the carriages containing twenty-four patients. Naval Ambulance Train No. 4 comprised only seven carriages, none with more than a maximum capacity of thirty-six wounded, the trailing load being lightened so as to reduce demands on engine power on the Highland main line. Also taken into account was the fact that the Scottish company's loading gauge was nearly a foot more restrictive than, for example, the Midland's.

It was, in any event, a curious decision considering that two of the UK's most important naval bases in this war – Scapa Flow and Invergordon – were serviced exclusively by the Highland. Indeed, when the 674 wounded from the Battle of Jutland were landed in Scotland in June 1916, the bulk of them came through Invergordon, and two special trains were started within twenty-four hours. Only two twelve-coach rakes could have accommodated such a number, so the term 'wounded' may have included those who had survived sinkings and who could travel in normal stock. (Incidentally, a requisitioned railway steamer, the South Eastern's *Engadine*, landed some 700 Jutland survivors further south at Rosyth and these do not seem to have been regarded as casualties.) In the light of such surely predictable events, there might have been a case for creating a naval hospital in the north of Scotland, although one was established in the central belt, with a conversion of a psychiatric hospital at Larbert into a 1,200-bed facility. As for the Highland main line, Edwin Pratt was scathing about the failure of the authorities to order and finance the doubling of the single line between Perth and Inverness before the war, making a stark comparison with the German preparations to facilitate troop movements by rail.

Two Scottish companies that had somewhat negative experiences when supplying the forces' medical services were the North British and the Great North of Scotland. The former was contacted directly by Scottish Command at Edinburgh Castle on the 6th – the day when the Cabinet debated whether or not to send the BEF to the Continent – and was ordered to provide an ambulance train within twenty-four hours. Supervised by company chairman William Whitelaw himself, the NB provided a vestibuled formation with capacity for ninety-six cots, and within the severe deadline. Unfortunately, and for no obvious reason, the new train was designed for hammock accommodation, and it is no surprise to learn that the Army declared this surplus to requirements by October 1915. Fortunately, the Royal Navy then took it over.

The GNSR had an even more unfortunate experience in trying to 'do its bit' for the cause. Again on the 6th, an order was received 'under conditions of great urgency' for an ambulance train 'of a very primitive kind indeed' according to contemporary historian Edwin Pratt. Within the now-usual breakneck schedule, the company apparently provided a non-corridor rake but with holes cut through compartment walls allowing staff to squeeze through the 3-foot-by-2-foot gaps, even if it involved clambering over the patients. Eight company joiners worked on this extraordinary conversion while the stock was en route from Inverurie for delivery at Inverness, completing their task shortly after arrival. This order had come from two individual naval officers, seemingly acting on their own initiative, and was a thoroughly unsatisfactory provision, although the company had responded with commendable purpose. Not surprisingly, the vehicles were converted back into normal stock within a year, and there is no reference to this incident in the company's board minutes. Additionally, the GNSR's Annual

Report for 1915 carries sixteen redactions, as they would be called nowadays, at the request of the Board of Trade.

Other companies constructing ambulance trains, without apparent commissioning difficulties, included the Great Central, which completed two ten-coach rakes within twelve days of an order on 14 August. A third was delivered in the following year, with another for the US Army in April 1918. Meanwhile at Swindon, the Great Western would turn out no fewer than twelve trains, four of them exclusively for use in the UK. Three of these were exhibited to the public at Paddington, Birmingham, and Bristol, and, despite their possibly macabre appearance, raised the considerable sum of £2,600 for military charities. At Newton Heath, the Lancashire & Yorkshire constructed eight ambulance trains without difficulties. On 'England's Military Railway', an eight-coach ambulance train was turned out in the earliest days of the war at the instigation of Lord Michelham, with a 'standard' train built later in the conflict by the L&SWR.

Building ambulance trains was not the only challenge they posed – loading and unloading them was a continuing problem. There are references in contemporary reports to contractors having to be brought in to unload troop trains, simply because porters were becoming scarcer (and apparently weaker), while in January 1917 it was even decreed that passengers must restrict the amount of luggage they carried as they could expect no assistance with it on railway premises. A touching portering story comes from the Lancashire & Yorkshire, a company which conveyed some 800 ambulance trains during the time of the war up until April 1919, mainly to hospitals at Liverpool (Aintree) and Halifax. It appears that ambulance trains would reach the corresponding L&Y stations either early in the morning or late in the evening, resulting in local staff unloading the trains and assisting the wounded – in their own free time. While admirable, this does suggest poor management, a failure to anticipate the logistical challenge posed by a passenger train whose passengers could not alight by themselves.

* * *

But the railway works, such as those of the Great Western, L&NWR, Midland, and North Eastern, where more than 40,000 were employed, went over to military manufacturing to a greater or lesser extent within a month of war's outbreak. This should have come as no surprise – the railways controlled most of the largest engineering factories in the country, and even those which might be seen as their rivals in terms of size, turnover, and staffing would struggle to equal the *variety* of production which railways could offer. A large company would construct not only its own locomotives, but the carriages of its trains, including soft furnishings, as well as the rails on which the trains ran.

The first such order was for ambulance trains for the RN, and, as we have seen, there was such (unwelcome and ill-advised) variety in their commissioning to begin with that in 1915 the *Railway Yearbook* had to annotate its listing of these trains with such comments as 'hurriedly prepared for immediate use and less elaborate than the others' – this related to the South Eastern & Chatham and Great North of Scotland's output, produced in record time by these patriotic companies, but misconceived in design. Stretchers were soon urgently required, with the REC acting as a clearing house for such orders.

* * *

It was becoming obvious that some measure would be necessary to assess how military demands could best be tackled by company works, with the REC assigning orders to ensure even distribution of work – and, not least, income. Standardised charging was introduced, basically little more than 'at cost', but, perhaps not surprisingly, many railways were to find difficulty in meeting their own engineering requirements over the next few years. No wonder that locomotive historian Campbell Highet records that 'engines had to be kept at work for long periods after they were normally due for shopping, and many boilers were worn out and working at reduced pressures'. Towards the end of the war, supplies of copper and steel varied in quantity, the former metal being severely rationed, for firebox repairs only, while steel was comparatively unlimited, although exclusively for commercial builders initially.

By October 1914 the REC had established a Railway War Manufacturers' Committee, comprising senior military officers and company heads. The latter included such illustrious CMEs as Bowen-Cooke, Churchward, Fowler, Gresley, and Hughes. While the capacity of the companies' works was impressive, it should be remembered that their efficiency depended on the skills of their workforces and the quantity of workers – these varied from 1,255 in the case of the Glasgow & South Western to 8,046 at Darlington and Gateshead (North Eastern), 8,288 at Derby (Midland Railway), 11,700 at Swindon, and no fewer than 14,800 at Crewe, Wolverton, and Earlstown (L&NWR). More orders followed before autumn had run its course, the first of them for 5,000 General Service wagons for artillery support. This was divided among no fewer than twenty-two companies, including one in Ireland, the first of these vehicles being turned out in December and the order completed by the end of January. Another 4,300 wagons were ordered almost immediately, along with another stretcher order, bringing the number supplied of the latter up to 25,195.

Clearly, the demand for stretchers had been underestimated.

In Case of Invasion

Compared to the Second World War, invasion does not loom large in volumes of British history of the first conflict. After overwhelming France and the

Low Countries with its Blitzkrieg in 1940, the German Army was logistically unprepared for what would have to have been the greatest opposed landing in history. Nevertheless, invasion seemed a real prospect at the time, with the Battle of Britain taking place in the skies above a nation in the throes of emergency, with the newly formed Home Guard parading with broomsticks.

But while 1914 can hardly compare with 1940 in terms of imminent invasion, nevertheless, before the end of the former year, contingency plans had to be made to repel a possible invasion, and needless to say, this involved Britain's railway companies.

* * *

At six o'clock on the evening of 16 November 1914, an order was issued to railways in central England to start immediate preparations for a troop movement requiring no fewer than 840 trains. One company alone was ordered to prepare 136 for immediate use. 'Prepare to repel an invasion' was the order of the day.

Even major histories of the First World War hardly mention this crisis, although transport historian Edwin Pratt recorded details in his book *British Railways in the Great War*. While he realised the enormity of this order in operational terms, Pratt did not name the company challenged, or by which Army headquarters. It seems probable that the order came from Western Command at Chester, liaising with its 'Secretary' railway, the London & North Western, which was the unfortunate company asked to shoulder the greatest part of this unexpected burden.

In the autumn of 1914, the authorities were alarmed by the efficient manner in which the German enemy had overcome Belgium, and particularly the temporary capital and port of Antwerp. All this despite the best efforts of that country's army, backed by British forces led by the Royal Naval Division and personally witnessed by the First Lord of the Admiralty, Winston Churchill. Antwerp was captured on 9 October, the last ships to leave having been two Great Eastern Railway steamers, the *Amsterdam* and the *Brussels*, thronged with Belgian refugees desperate to escape.

* * *

By the end of October, Allied forces had managed to halt the enemy's drive towards the Channel ports of Dunkirk and Calais, but London can hardly have felt reassured by all this enemy activity, and it must have seemed equally possible that an invasion of Britain might now be undertaken from Belgian soil. The BEF initially sent to France in August might be tiny by European standards – 50,000 men compared to Germany's potential of 2.3 million on its Western Front – but in October this left Britain desperately short of trained troops. In the words of historian Hew Strachan, 'Kitchener no longer had two regular divisions [left in the UK], and he did not trust the Territorials. The Admiralty was therefore constrained to cover the East Coast.' This was done by thinning out units of the Grand Fleet to ports from Tyneside to Essex, but battlecruisers had already been despatched to the South Atlantic to avenge the defeat at Coronel. Making the Army's job even more daunting was the realisation that the digging of defensive positions on both sides on the Continent would release experienced offensive units, what Strachan calls 'a disposable land force'.

This could explain the panic evident in the orders given the railways in mid-November, with preparations to be made for an eastward move of forces to coastal areas along sections of the coast from the Forth to the Thames. The panic was inflamed by the German Navy's ability to shell such towns as Great Yarmouth on 3 November, later followed by Hartlepool and Scarborough. At the former of these two towns, 'the North Eastern [Railway] was somewhat knocked about', records historian Hamilton Ellis, in a rather flippant summing-up of a deadly attack on a civilian target, and one not mentioned in Edwin Pratt's otherwise comprehensive work. In the words of historian Richard Lacey:

> Both Hartlepool and West Hartlepool were targeted – they were separate towns at the time, not being unified until 1967. Two NER employees were killed while at work, and there was substantial damage to wagons, track and telegraph wires in the docks area, as well as to two cranes, a water column, a coal elevator, two locomotives and West Hartlepool engine shed itself. The bombardment is very much a part of local history (there were at least 127 deaths including those occurring later from wounds). Whitby and Scarborough were both bombarded on the same day, and there was railway damage at both. At Whitby, one NER employee was killed, and there was some damage to the station's glass roof, a locomotive, a signal cabin and a carriage. Scarborough (where the railway is more inland) suffered only minor damage to the roof of the excursion station.

Nevertheless, the last-named town suffered ninety-three deaths and nearly 500 wounded, and, as if unsated, the enemy returned in September 1917. On this later occasion a U-boat fired thirty shells, apparently at the castle, but also damaged platform 1 at the Central station. Three civilians were killed and six injured. Meanwhile, the Grand Fleet – the greatest the world had ever seen – swung at anchor hundreds of miles to the north in Scapa Flow. It had even been moved temporarily to Northern Irish waters towards the end of October 1914 to preserve it from German submarines. As a result those RN vessels which could still be mustered in the North Sea very nearly lost a partial engagement at Dogger Bank in the following month.

Incidentally, 'civil defence' advice given to the citizens of such towns as Dover was wildly inappropriate. Inhabitants of the port were advised to take to the high ground behind the town in the event of a bombardment – perhaps an unconscious tribute to the accuracy of German range finding, but nevertheless reckless advice. In a raid on 21 and 22 December 1917, a bombardment by enemy battlecruisers targeted, either by error or design, the exact area specified by the authorities as 'safe'. Draft notices bearing the ominous message 'Transport by rail for refugees could not be guaranteed' were prepared for sending to local authorities, such as Dover, on the east and south coasts, but fortunately only saw the light of day in the pages of Edwin Pratt's admirable study.

Steps were already being taken to guarantee the safety of the railways themselves. On 26 October, the REC circulated details of the 'guarding of lines', dividing these into primary and secondary importance. No actual company or railway was specified, with the exception of 'some colliery lines in South Wales' clearly considered of primary importance. Railways in this category were to be patrolled by soldiers, secondary lines by Territorials and reservists. Some 'structures', presumably tunnels and bridges, were to be guarded by 'National Reservists' – their identity being unclear – and all civilian watchmen were to be withdrawn in such cases, probably in case they were arrested (or worse) by mistake. Details of assignments were to be agreed with the relevant Army Command Centre, and the inference to be drawn from Circular 120 was that the railway companies were responsible for initiating these defensive measures themselves. But the Highland lines to the Far North were considered so important that no fewer than twenty-five bridges and tunnels were guarded – by the military – on the route north of Perth, with footplate crews instructed to sound their whistles when approaching.

***

But there was nothing half-hearted about the Army's requirements in November 1914. The 840 trains were to be composed of stock displaying what was later described as high 'route availability', and, depending on whether needed for passenger or livestock transport, were to be composed of sixteen to thirty-four vehicles each, assembled in any of twenty prearranged formations. All this comprised a total of anything between 13,500 to 28,000 carriages and wagons, none of which could be used more than once in this operation. These were to be (literally) sidelined straight away in an area of the Midlands all the way across to North Wales, while the enemy was awaited.

Within two years, even more bureaucratic instructions on train assembly had been drawn up, along with description of routes, 'assembly' and 'change' stations, and new command structures. The make-up of the rakes was reduced from twenty varieties to just five, ranging from a train with sixty-five passenger compartments and five cattle trucks to the opposite extent, fifteen compartments and twenty-one trucks. Each truck should house eight horses, or forty men in some circumstances, and historian Christian Wolmer points out that the ratio 8/40 became a recognised standard for passengers and stock in the next war, and on both sides. Tommies called this 'Omms and Chevoos'! But this is a surely unique instance of British soldiers being expected to travel in livestock vehicles in the UK, with Edwin Pratt recording that 'a shortage of third class coaches might make it necessary that some of the men should travel in cattle trucks'. This was in sharp contrast to the mere 200 troops transported in an entire train when the BEF first went to war. In any event, the concept of combining an infantry battalion with its own horse-drawn vehicles was outmoded, as we have seen.

* * *

Looking back, one is forced to wonder what troops these trains were expected to transport within the UK in late 1914. The huge number of volunteers would not achieve full readiness until forming the 'New Army' in the next spring, and Canadian troops were not yet available. Pratt suggests that this sidelining (the 'standing idle of rolling-stock') took place over a period of two years, in the case of seventy such train formations, by which time the plan for defending the UK's soil had changed. With the immediate crisis of November 1914 over, plans were now focused on a Central England Camp, strategically placed so that an army could be transported quickly from it to any invasion site. These plans were detailed, and were – unusually – made available to Edwin Pratt as an example of how well the authorities were prepared, or so they thought.

Detailed but not altogether straightforward planning developed regarding telegraph lines – how and when to cut them, and to what extent that would cripple railway communications even more than the enemy's, assuming that one of the invader's priorities was to break into Post Office telegraphs. These were just some of the contingency arrangements which, unlike Germany's Schlieffen Plan, would never be put into effect.

Arrangements for loading troops on to their transports were complicated to say the least, with what would normally be called junction stations being renamed 'collection' points – for example, Carlisle – and these would be expected to assemble and despatch troops from up to two hours' rail journey away. This was presumably so that prescribed vehicles and train rakes would be used in approaching the area of conflict, but effectively meant using two different trains for the same battalion of troops, with all the potential for confusion in transferring from one train to another. As it was, there were guidelines laid down for water stops, specifying the number of standpipes for soldiers to fill their bottles and for horses to be watered, no stoppage to be more than thirty minutes in length. Trains would all start their journeys theoretically at 00.00 on the twenty-four-hour clock. Pratt assumed that this was noon, which is not the modern interpretation, but he may have been unaware that effectively the operations were being timed on an 'elapsed' basis.

Controlling all this was a command structure divided into 'Forward' and 'Rearward' centres. In the former category were the Scottish, Northern, and Eastern Army commands, indicating on which coastline the enemy was expected. York-based Northern Command was sub-divided into three areas, stretching altogether from the Tweed to south of the Humber, with Eastern supervising troop delivery to the coast between the Wash and Kent. (Presumably the coast between Grimsby and Skegness was left to its own devices.) Southern and Western commands were 'Rearward', as was the Aldershot area. It appears that the London & North Western was the Army's liaison company in administering the Central Force, linking with Western Command, and – for the first two months of the war – Eastern Command as well. This would have given the railway managers a good understanding of regional problems and help establish vital contacts. It may be that the appointment of the South Eastern & Chatham as Eastern Command's Secretary Company had been short-sighted, and was founded on the assumption that no enemy would impugn Belgian neutrality, the subject of a long-standing treaty. Consequently, there would be no hostile harbours or naval bases south of the Low Countries' border with Germany, and the loss of Antwerp and Zeebrugge must have been a shock to London as well as the unfortunate Belgians. As it was, the Great Eastern, or the otherwise comparatively untroubled Great Northern, might have made a more appropriate, or at least appropriately-located Secretary company.

While all this may seem complicated, it was based on the reasonable assumption that it was preferable to maintain only light forces on the coastline and await a clear identification of the enemy's main 'push' before committing defenders in number. Exactly such an approach was suggested by General Sir Alan Brooke (later Lord Alanbrooke) in the next war, when facing the prospect of a Nazi invasion in 1940, and this earned him promotion over an older commander (General Ironside) who had clearly forgotten the plan of 1916. The Germans themselves planned such a defensive strategy to combat the Allied landings in France in 1944, but the Panzers, kept back from the coast, could not be unleashed coastwards in time, allegedly because no-one dared to wake the sleeping Hitler. So, the theory behind a 'central England camp' in 1916, with all the attendant logistical nightmares it would pose for Britain's railways, was nevertheless a sound one.

* * *

In the eighteen months after the invasion scare of November 1914, it was decided to build two armoured trains to move and operate artillery wherever they were needed on coastal lines. The trains were very much a co-operative venture among the companies. The guns were mounted on wagon chassis from the Caledonian, with infantry support vehicles – 40-ton coal wagons roofed and supplied by the Great Western – powered by a GNR locomotive, and the final assembly carried out by the LN&W at Crewe.

These metallic monsters were powered by Great Northern 0-6-2 class N1 locomotives, acquired by the War Office in December 1914 and March 1915 respectively for a total of £6,000. After being armoured, they were christened with the names *Norna* and *Alice*, and were required to maintain steam at all times. A further locomotive was loaned to the War Office during the autumn of 1917. The two original locomotives would be bought back by the new LNER in March 1923.

The armour was presumably thought necessary to protect the stock and its crew from enemy ships close enough to shore to be able to identify any source of return fire. The ships would *have* to be close – the train's 12-pounders had a range of only 3 miles, while even Germany's older battleships could fire easily at 10 miles' range, the optimum level of visibility on 90 per cent of days in the North Sea. No. 1 armoured train was stationed at North Walsham, on a section of joint GER/M&GNR line which would give immediate access to the coast from Sheringham south to Lowestoft. No. 2 was located at St Margaret's in Edinburgh for the defence of the Berwickshire and Fife coasts, although one would imagine that the nearness of Rosyth naval base, and the well-armed islands guarding it, would have made an attack on the Forth unlikely. A Zeppelin raid in April 1916 was easily repelled by shore and naval batteries, but with no help from Armoured Train No. 2.

One suspects that the trains were intended primarily for psychological effect, and would be difficult to operate. Not the least of the problems would be the need for the locomotive to be kept permanently in steam. This would be impossible in practical terms, with boiler washouts being necessary probably at least every fortnight. The fire would also have to be cleaned regularly. Presumably, this kind of essential maintenance could be carried out overnight, although in theory a coastal bombardment was just as much a prospect as during daylight, and using starshell, the marauders could illuminate a sleeping town. Exactly this happened at Dover in December 1917, and even if an armoured train had been stationed in the vicinity, it might very well have been unable to locate the bombarding ships. Interestingly, during the 1926 General Strike, it was decided that a rail-mounted armoured car should patrol north and south of Newcastle, although it was not Germans being targeted on that occasion.

The threat of invasion was officially laid to rest by the end of 1917, when the Admiralty agreed with Army commanders that the Germans were unlikely to secure a landing for 70,000 men on the eastern side of England with less than thirty-six hours' warning, and that even enemy naval exercises in the Baltic could be predicted in advance. Even so, the Dover bombardment by capital ships was still to come. By the end of the conflict, 570 civilians and servicemen had been killed on home soil by enemy action, exactly one-tenth of them by bombardment rather than by bombing from the air.

In considering the 1914 invasion scare, and the more measured response in 1916 of the Central England Camp, it is difficult to assess how seriously the German invasion threat was viewed. Nobody doubted the invincibility of the Royal Navy, and popular agitation ('Jingoism') in the five years before war was declared had ensured that naval forces were constantly renewed and strengthened. So, while the authorities may have had reason to panic when the coastal bombardments began in 1914, it is doubtful if the average man in the street, or more pertinently in this case, the average railwayman, volunteered for the armed forces through any sense of national preservation. Occupational boredom or dislike of working pay and conditions were surely more likely motivations. If the war was popularly expected to be 'over by Christmas' (and the REC believed a resolution was possible before the end of the following year), it was expected to conclude with British troops in Berlin.

New Traffic Streams I

'La Marseillaise' was sung on one station platform, 'Deutschland, Deutschland, über alles' on another. This was the astonishing sight and sound at Charing Cross station in the summer of 1914 as French and German Army reservists began their homeward journeys from London before Britain had even declared war. It was an early indication for one of the six railway companies liaising with Army command centres – in this case, the South Eastern & Chatham – that the next four years and three months were to be like no other time in British history. And the transport of rival reservists was only the beginning.

While there was to be no shortage of new traffic on the railways in the next five years, there was a surprising continuation of existing passenger operations. Perhaps this should not be a revelation, given the REC's policy of 'business as usual', particularly as far as excursion traffic is concerned, but all this is worth more than a passing mention.

The war had been under way for some six months when, for example, the Great Western drew up its advertising campaign for the following summer, and so the 1915 *Railway Yearbook* carried a full-page advertisement for the GWR as 'The Holiday Line'. While this was not repeated in 1916, it was in the latter year that the company found itself running the Cornish Riviera express in three sections one day in late July, to carry more than 2,000 passengers who wished to avail themselves of a holiday in Devon or Cornwall. This was the month when the Somme offensive began, including the day when the British Army suffered its worst-ever casualty statistic.

By 1919 the only holiday adverts carried in the *Railway Yearbook* were for three small rail companies – the Belfast & County Down, Isle of Wight Central, and the Maryport & Carlisle. While extolling the scenery their networks accessed, only one company pictured what the public were now missing – namely the Maryport, illustrating their services with a plate of Crummock Water. Meanwhile, the GWR offered sites for 'Works and warehouses', and there were many new potential sources of traffic to challenge the railways' ability to support the war effort.

* * *

While the BEF found its way to France with little assistance from the REC, the latter organisation busied itself with problems resulting. Circular 55, sent out to the companies on 31 August, was concerned with the transport of parcels to the BEF and Royal Navy. These were to be carried free of charge by the railways provided they came from recognised military associations or charities, and were not addressed to any particular unit or individual. Containing 'comforts', these could comprise woollens, reading matter, or items less personal than those sent by relatives to their loved ones in the trenches or at sea, and which would have to be paid for, as was made clear in Circular 62.

The scale of parcel transport is jaw-dropping. One might imagine that the Army could supply basic toiletries for its troops, but even food was a problem. While anecdotal evidence suggests that Germans suffered more from food shortages than British soldiers, possibly because the latter's fighting defensively ensured shorter supply lines, letters home to 'Blighty' requested not only chocolate, but such 'luxury' items as razor blades and soap. As a result, posted parcels became a major daily traffic. From 11.00 every morning a van train was assembled at Victoria, being filled throughout the day until 23.30, with a limit of thirty-five vehicles. If this was exceeded, the train was run to the Channel ports in two sections. In the final four months of 1914, the number of sacks totalled 25,785. It increased year on year, with a maximum of 4,210,805 sacks in 1917, dropping to 3,026,173 in the final year of war. Total weight of this cargo was 324,596 tons.

These figures do not include mail for POWs in Germany – this was carried by Great Eastern trains and steamers. When the steamer *Colchester* was taken by German forces in 1916, the British newspapers were exercised by the fate of the mails, and whether the Germans would allow their continued passage. Journalists might equally have asked how a railway steamer being 'escorted' by British destroyers could have been captured in the first place, a matter discussed more fully later in this book.

* * *

One of these new traffic generators was described, subtly, in an REC Circular in mid-April 1915. The committee distributed guidelines on the free transport of soldiers' and sailors' corpses, the paperwork for which was to be kept well away from the public's eyes. It was surely only a coincidence that this circular was issued in the same month that the Gladstone family had been able to have the former Prime Minister's grandson exhumed from a battlefield grave and taken to the family plot in Cheshire. This took place with the consent of King and Prime Minister, but the Army authorities were alarmed by this action, one scarcely open to every grieving family, but nevertheless a precedent in a war where even the least visionary commander could see that moving bodies homewards was likely to present an enormous logistical problem, as well as having an obviously damaging effect on Army morale.

By the following autumn it had been decided that those who fell in battle would be buried on the Continent in what became Imperial, and later Commonwealth, War Graves. This proved to be controversial, the lack of class distinction among the white crosses being the opposite of the hierarchical nature of British society at the time, and too egalitarian for many critics. But a sense of dignified equality prevailed, resulting in the huge graveyards which are such a feature of the Flanders landscape today, and, with naval dead being buried at sea, the REC guidelines would be used only for the transport of the dead within the UK, usually from hospital to the family's choice of graveyard. Unfortunately, even this seemingly simple transaction became more complicated following the Battle of the Somme, as will be related later.

* * *

There were two new traffic streams which were entirely a product of war, but less macabre than the above. Britain's Grand Fleet was sent to Scapa Flow in Orkney at the beginning of war, in order to interdict any attempt by the German High Seas Fleet to reach the Atlantic. With overpowering numerical superiority, the British fleet was believed invincible, but this ensured that the smaller enemy fleet did no more than swing at anchor for most of the war. By not engaging the Grand Fleet, the German Navy could ensure that a large concentration of smaller support vessels, particularly destroyers, would be condemned to comparative inaction awaiting escort duties with the battleships, and not engage in aggressive actions in German waters. Indeed, in one of the few which did take place two South Eastern turbine steamers took an active part. But the presence of the Grand Fleet so far north created two new traffic streams – in carrying men, and coal.

Unfortunately, British capital ships, with the exception of the brand-new Queen Elizabeth class battleships, were coal-fired. It would seem logical, and comparatively easy, to transport the coal to Orkney by coastal vessel, and there were plenty of colliers in the merchant fleet, as Britain was a major exporter of coal. (This did not of course apply to Ireland, which was one of the markets for it.) But early U-boat activity in the Channel – specifically the sinking of three British cruisers in September 1914 – horrified the Admiralty, and it was clear that the submarine menace had been underestimated. The coal – and South Wales produced the most suitable for naval furnaces – was going to have to travel most of the way by rail.

* * *

Coal being hauled northwards from South Wales was heading for any one of a number of destinations, but in the case of fuel for the capital ships, it was obvious that it would have to be transferred to a coasting vessel sooner or later, and preferably the latter. The best port for this soon emerged as Grangemouth, the deep-water port farthest inland in the Firth of Forth, some 10 miles west of the Forth Bridge. Taken over by Government from 13 November 1914, the docks and neighbouring canal were owned and serviced by the Caledonian Railway, although that company required running powers over the North British to reach this, probably Scotland's most modern port. As recently as 1906, hydraulic coal hoists had been commissioned, capable of lifting and emptying a wagon and load of up to 35 tons from a height of 50 feet above sea level into a vessel below. Two hatches could be filled simultaneously, with a turnaround at each hoist of fifty wagons each hour, and the dock accommodated ships of up to 30-foot draught. An older dock also had four hoists and the company's investment was clearly bearing fruit as the war broadened out.

Other East Coast ports were also geared to coal-exporting – the North Eastern carried 34 million tons of locally mined coal in 1916, much of it for export – while the North British moved about half that amount, through Leith and two of the Fife ports. Some coal could be moved farther north, to Invergordon, where there were repair facilities. But in many cases, at the end of this channel of fuel supply, no matter how modern the trans-shipment had been at Grangemouth, was a human chain of men passing along pails of coal to empty into the chute of an ironclad, a lengthy, filthy, ordeal hated by every seaman.

But this did not entirely eliminate the problem posed by the U-boats, for whom the Forth was a happy hunting ground. As late as January 1918, a submarine scare – almost certainly a false alarm – contributed to a British naval manoeuvre which went horribly wrong, resulting in the loss of two K-class submarines, sunk by RN ships with the death of 105 men. This was known, with grim irony, as the Battle of the Isle of May. A port on the west coast equipped with mechanised coal loading and well away from U-boat activity, at least initially, would have been preferable.

On 27 August 1914, the first northbound coal train began to wend its way from the Welsh coalfield through Pontypool Road, all the way on GWR tracks on to a joint line to Warrington, where the L&NWR took over. Carlisle would normally be the next company handover point, but in fact some trains made their way via Blackburn on the L&Y to Hellifield, for the Midland to move over the Settle & Carlisle. This was to prevent the West Coast Main Line being congested with too much slow-moving traffic, and this could be avoided at Carlisle, where some of these workings proceeded north via the Glasgow & South Western or North British, in addition to the obvious working by Caledonian.

The sheer number of these workings was considerable – 13,361 up until the end of 1918. Assuming each comprised forty wagons of 10 tons' capacity, this cumulated as 5.45 million tons of fuel. Even though the wagons concerned were hand-braked, necessitating a slow pace, it proved possible to move a train load from Pontypool to Grangemouth in less than forty-eight hours. Historian Edwin Pratt records that this was carried 'free, under government guarantee' – effectively free but with the participating companies receiving payment in quarterly instalments. The port also processed 220,000 tons of fuel oil for the naval base at Rosyth, most of it delivered by ship to the west coast and then taken by the (Caledonian Railway's) Forth & Clyde Canal from Bowling, and when that proved too time-consuming, by newly constructed pipeline along the canalside to Grangemouth.

By 1918, coal would have to be exported to France, as so much of that nation's coalfield was now occupied by another nation. The other commodity requiring transport to, and from, the Far North was human.

* * *

The RN complement stationed at Scapa Flow in the Orkney islands ran into tens of thousands if ships' crews are included. Their posting was almost as far removed from the centres of population as it was possible to be in the UK. With the Grand Fleet regarded as the principal bulwark protecting this nation, it is surprising indeed that, for so much of the war, there was no scheduled train to convey naval personnel between the cities of the south and Thurso, ferry port for Orkney on the Pentland Firth.

It was only in February 1917, fully nine months after the Battle of Jutland, that it was decided to create a regular six-days-a-week service to and from Euston and the WCML to Perth and then ever northwards on the Highland Railway. Previously, naval officers and ratings had been expected to make this marathon journey on their own – no easy matter for sailors from working-class families who may never have been far from their hometowns. Edwin Pratt lists the problems encountered by these men – including becoming 'stranded at towns or junctions on route', or even worse, 'drifting into bad company'. Surprisingly, there were some reports of 'altercations' with civilians, and even sailors travelling under arrest and escort would be transported by passenger train (and their fares not covered by the guaranteed profit agreement of 1914; see 'The Railways Commanded II').

The solution was the Navy Train, perhaps a unique hybrid of a timetabled service and a 'special'. Comprising fourteen vehicles, this departed Euston five evenings a week at 1800 hours, except in winter, when a 15.00 departure would ensure embarkation at Thurso during daylight the next day. Connections with South Wales and Devon were accomplished at Crewe, and with Tyneside and Yorkshire at Carlisle. The route covered 717 miles in 1,290 minutes northbound and fifty minutes more in the Up direction. The use of corridor stock meant that a master-at-arms could patrol the vehicles, and only officers would be allowed sleepers. 'Bag' meals were provided at various major stations, but at Inverness even officers would be denied a sit-down meal if the train was late (not an inconceivable occurrence). Pratt commented that officers could then have only a whisky or a cup of tea, but not both. The train was open to Army and RFC/RAF personnel by arrangement, and even women could be accommodated, but only if serving with the Wrens or nursing services. Up to thirty-five prisoners could be transported in locked compartments. From May 1917 the North British assumed the Caledonian's responsibility for taking over from the L&NW at Carlisle, and the Waverley Route was followed northwards. This was to allow a stop at Inverkeithing, near to Rosyth, soon to be the major base for most of the Grand Fleet – previously there had to be a 'backwards' journey down from Perth. From the latter point, a third company took over the workings.

This was of course the Highland Railway, whose route ran northwards from Perth up the central spine of Scotland to Inverness. From here it wended its way to Dingwall, a branch going off (and thankfully still does) to Kyle of Lochalsh. The main line, if a single track can be so called, continued to the naval base of Invergordon, and then, by a route made lengthier by the need to divert inland to avoid crossing the Dornoch Firth, to the Far North. Even the most part of the Perth–Inverness route was single, apart from the northbound climb – over 20 miles – from Blair Atholl to the summit at Drumochter, 1,484 feet above sea level and the highest point in the UK where express passenger trains were operated. Even this was not the end of the climbing, with challenging inclines on the two (again, single-line) routes north from Aviemore to Inverness. The author's father made this journey several times as a serviceman and was astounded at how slow it all was – and that was in the next war.

Locomotive power had already proved a major problem for the Highland. As early as August 1915 the company's officials, including the CME, Frederic Smith, had met REC representatives at Perth to highlight the loss of motive power. Of 152 main-line locomotives, fifty were out of commission awaiting repair and fifty more were being operated while in need of it. A loan of twenty engines was immediately arranged, and it was believed that the pressure would ease with the imminent introduction of Smith's River class of 4-6-0s. While these proved to be excellent engines, they did so on a different railway – the Caledonian, to whom they were sold (at a profit) when the Rivers proved to have been designed without full consultation with the line's engineer and were unusable. Smith's resignation was requested and received, and the Highland struggled on as best it could.

Perhaps surprisingly, the service was only once a victim of extreme weather, but once was quite enough. In January 1918 the northbound Navy Train became embedded in snow 8 miles south of Thurso, and remained there *for a week*. Three snowploughs were also trapped. Naval staff were fit enough to be able to walk to town to continue their marathon journey, and enable the companies to claim that they had safely delivered, by April of the following year, nearly half a million servicemen and women.

Edwin Pratt was not backward in condemning successive British governments for failing to realise the strategic value of the Highland Railway after Admiral Fisher had announced his 'discovery' of Scapa Flow in 1905. The Russians had doubled their lines running westwards, and received French financial help in doing so, thus undermining the Schlieffen Plan by forcing the German High Command to hurriedly transfer two divisions to the east, so why could the Highland not be subsidised in improving its route northwards? One suspects that the answer was the assumption that there was no need to.

* * *

The north and north-west of Scotland became so important for strategic reasons that the REC announced in July 1916 that the whole area – normally a playground in August for the better-off classes of society – was now a Special Military Area and a permit would be necessary for entry. Circular 622 imposed a ban on through booking by rail, although this was slightly eased in 632, possibly because of the short notice given. Highland historian D.L.G. Hunter recorded that all passenger workings into Inverness had their doors locked before leaving the last station prior to the Highland capital, 'so that passengers could be detrained under control'.

In any event, the Highland Railway was finding two of its branches a source of Government attention. The line from Dingwall to Strathpeffer and Kyle began to enter the busiest period in its history, never more so than when American-manufactured mines needed to be moved across the country to North Sea bases. Passenger services were restricted to one working each way daily. But the Inverness Harbour branch became something of a headache, not least because it did not exist before the war. The company knew that the Admiralty wanted to

First a general and then Field Marshal in the First World War, Sir Douglas Haig finally delivered victory in November 1918, but at appalling costs in number of lives lost. He bizarrely invited the principal members of the Railway Executive Committee to visit the Somme battlefield just as the battle was drawing to an end in bloody stalemate in November 1916. This bronze equestrian statue of Haig by G. E. Wade has been so frequently vandalised that it has had to be moved to an inner court in Edinburgh Castle.

A granite Celtic cross commemorates the Quintinshill disaster of May 1915 with, in the wall behind, the names of the 227 victims of the Royal Scots regiment, mainly from Leith. Unfortunately, a notice at the Rosebank cemetery in Pilrig, Edinburgh, exhibits the wrong date of the disaster.

Sir Herbert Walker became Acting Chairman of the Railway Executive Committee following the death of Sir Frank Ree, just four months before the First World War began. Walker had been assistant to Ree at the L&NWR, and had served the company for twenty-six years before being appointed GM of the London & South Western in 1912.

SPECIAL RAILWAY NOTICE

PASSENGERS' LUGGAGE.

OWING TO THE ENLISTMENT OF RAILWAYMEN, AND THE CONSEQUENT SHORTAGE OF STAFF, THE RAILWAY COMPANIES EARNESTLY REQUEST PASSENGERS TO LIMIT THE QUANTITY OF LUGGAGE AS MUCH AS POSSIBLE.

By Order of the
RAILWAY EXECUTIVE COMMITTEE.

Portering became a major problem for Britain's railways as the war went on. No arrangements had been implemented to unload ambulance trains at stations close to military hospitals, and so many railwaymen had enlisted by 1917 that the travelling public had to observe a 100-lb limit on personal luggage, to enable female porters to assist.

IMPORTANT RAILWAY NOTICE

NOTICE IS HEREBY GIVEN

that the following alterations in Passenger Train travel, as applying to the Railways in Great Britain, will come into force on and from 1st JANUARY, 1917:—

1. PASSENGER TRAIN SERVICES.
   The Passenger Train Services will be considerably curtailed and decelerated. For details see the Company's Time Tables and Notices.
2. RESERVATION OF SEATS, COMPARTMENTS, &c.
   The reservation of seats and compartments, and saloons for private parties, will be discontinued.
3. SLEEPING AND DINING CARS.
   The running of Sleeping and Dining Cars will be further curtailed.
4. THROUGH COACHES.
   The running of certain Slip Coaches and Through Coaches of Main Line Trains to Branch Lines will be discontinued.
5. PROHIBITION OF CONVEYANCE OF MOTOR CARS, CARRIAGES, &c.
   Road Vehicles, such as Motor Cars, Carriages, Show Vans, &c. will not be accepted for conveyance by Passenger Train.
6. INCREASE OF FARES.
   All Passenger Fares, except Workmen's Tickets (Daily and Weekly), Season, Traders' and Zone Tickets, will be increased by 50 per cent.
7. CANCELLATION OF REDUCED FARE FACILITIES.
   Reduced Fare facilities will in certain cases be discontinued. See Announcements by individual Companies.
8. INTER-AVAILABILITY OF TICKETS.
   Passengers holding Ordinary, Season, or Traders' Tickets covering points directly served by two or more Companies' Lines will be allowed to travel, for the throughout journey only, by any route as available.
   In cases where Through Tickets have been issued and there is no direct through service a passenger will be permitted to complete the journey by a recognised alternative route.
   These Arrangements will not apply to local residential services unless specially authorised.
9. LIMITATION IN WEIGHT OF LUGGAGE ACCOMPANYING PASSENGERS.
   The Railway Companies will not undertake to give assistance in the handling of Passengers' luggage.
   Subject to certain exceptions, the amount of ordinary personal luggage allowed free of charge will be 100 lbs. (irrespective of the class of ticket held), and NO PASSENGER WILL BE PERMITTED TO TAKE MORE THAN 100 LBS. WEIGHT OF LUGGAGE BY TRAIN.

By Order,
THE RAILWAY EXECUTIVE COMMITTEE.

London, December, 1916.

Following Haig's appeal to the REC to organise the transfer of so much railway material and equipment to the Continent, British train services had to be curtailed and in some cases withdrawn altogether. It was a tacit admission by the REC in 1917 that its policy of 'business as usual' was flawed.

Every British soldier arriving at Folkestone in this picture has a smile on his face, confirming that the First World War is over at last. Demobilisation was in fact a headache for the authorities, not least the railways, anxious to have important staff returned to them as soon as possible.

Soldiers embarking on a steamer en route to the Continent on an unknown date. No troopship was torpedoed or mined while en route, but at least two railway ships bringing wounded back to Blighty were sunk, with serious loss of life.

Women porters at Marylebone goods station, July 1917. From January of that year, passengers had been forbidden to carry more than 100 lbs of hand luggage, presumably so that women porters could assist without difficulty. Curiously, an exception had to be made for research scientists, who could not bear to be parted from equipment. (Courtesy of John Alsop)

The obviously impressive spit-and-polish job accomplished by these women engine cleaners on their Great Northern K2 locomotive would not earn them a war bonus. In December 1916 the GNR was one of ten companies which declined to offer women workers a wage supplement at a time when they could have earned far more working in munitions production. (Courtesy of John Alsop)

It was not surprising that London's underground railways, then privately owned, should seek female labour to replace male staff. The Metropolitan District saw a 110 per cent staff turnover, and the rival Metropolitan, some of whose workers are seen here, was almost certainly the same. It was the most profitable railway in the UK. (Courtesy of John Alsop)

Assembled at Crewe, two armoured trains each comprised two 12-pdr guns supported by GWR 40-ton wagons, and chassis work by the Caledonian. Motive power was supplied by GNR tank locomotives, although a tender is visible in this photograph. How effective this rail-mounted artillery would be, with a range of only 3 miles, was a moot question. (Courtesy of John Alsop)

Even with the Folkestone–Boulogne passage given over exclusively to the military from November 1915, there was still a need for a dedicated harbour on the Channel coast, so Richborough was commissioned and fully operational within two years. The 'cargo' seen awaiting transit includes tanks and ROD 2-8-0s, all of which would make crane handling very difficult, but train ferries would facilitate movement of them to and from France. (Courtesy of John Alsop)

Train ferries began working in and out of Richborough late in 1917, and from Southampton the following year. Here their versatile layout is seen, capable of handling road vehicles as well as railway wagons and locomotives. After the end of the war each vessel was taking 400 horses at a time when the French authorities asked for them to be returned to Blighty, no doubt because animal fodder was always such a precious commodity. (Courtesy of John Alsop)

'Hideous' is the description of the Richborough train ferries by ship historians, although nobody doubted their usefulness in the First World War, especially when tanks and locomotives had to be transported to France. All three operating here survived this war, but two of them were lost to enemy action in the next, one sinking with a cargo of locomotives in 1945. (Courtesy of John Alsop)

'Mons' and other emotive names were immortalised by the North British Railway when their C class 0-6-0s returned from later service on the Continent. Here No. 65224 is seen in BR days banking a goods train bound for the LMR (judging by the brake van) on the Waverley Route, once used by the Naval Special running daily between Euston and Thurso. (Courtesy of W. S. Sellar)

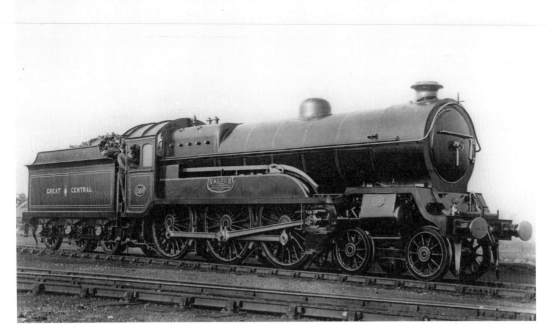

Naming a locomotive to commemorate railwaymen who gave their lives in the Great War seems so logical that it is surprising that it happened so rarely. Here a handsome 4-6-0 of the Great Central, named *Valour*, heads an express northwards out of London in the early 1920s, with the locomotive still in GCR livery. (Courtesy of John Alsop)

Train Ferry. Richborough.

Captain Charles Fryatt, who was killed by the Germans for defending his ship, the SS *Brussels*. He was following advice from the Admiralty – to ram a stopped U-boat – which was unrealistic and dangerous, and allowed the Germans to argue that civilian crews were acting aggresively. (J. & C. McCutcheon Collection)

The Captain C. A. Fryatt Memorial in Dovercourt churchyard near Harwich. Even the normally unemotional Herbert Asquith, in his final year as Prime Minister, was outraged by this 'execution'.(J. & C. McCutcheon Collection)

A Great Eastern Railway advertisement for trips on the *Brussels*. The Great Eastern Railway was expected to continue this important sea passage without armed protection, and with a fleet reduced by calls for minesweepers and troop support vessels. (J. & C. McCutcheon Collection)

The memorial to Great Eastern Railway employees killed in the war is located at London's Liverpool Street station. It was unveiled in June 1922 by General Sir Henry Wilson, who was assassinated by the IRA immediately on his return home. (J. & C. McCutcheon Collection)

British territorial soldiers guarding the railway near Rochester station on the SE&CR. Regular soldiers were used to guard railways of primary importance, and this line's proximity to Chatham might have qualified it for the highest level of security. The companies themselves were expected by the REC to arrange this with their nearest Army Command HQ, of which there were six in the UK. (J. & C. McCutcheon Collection)

A depiction of soldiers arriving in London on leave, and being welcomed by their families on their return home. (J. & C. McCutcheon Collection)

In contrast to the picture at the top of this page, the illustration above shows wives and parents saying goodbye to their relatives as they leave Victoria station to go to the Front. (J. & C. McCutcheon Collection)

Schoolboys from Eton line up along the platform at Didcot Junction, preparing to unload trains full of war supplies. (J. & C. McCutcheon Collection)

This armoured car, seen in the Guinness Brewery Yard in Dublin, was an improvisation made of locomotive smokeboxes. (J. & C. McCutcheon Collection)

Above: This illustration shows one group of soldiers preparing to board their train to the Front, while, on the opposite platform, a train full of wounded soldiers alight. (J. & C. McCutcheon Collection)

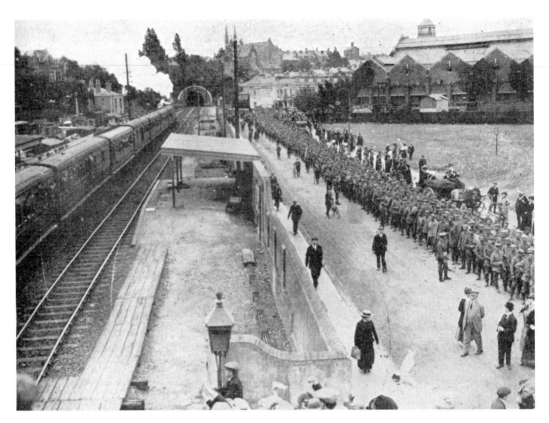

For them, the war was over. German POWs are seen in transit within the UK, their transport yet another task loaded on to the railways, when it might have been more appropriate to keep prisoners on the Continent. (J. & C. McCutcheon Collection)

Wounded soldiers, having got off their ambulance train, walk along the platform to receive treatment. (J. & C. McCutcheon Collection)

The Big Cranes

Huge cranes lift guns on to wagons for transportation. As the war progressed, the demand for the heaviest guns moved from the Royal Navy to the Army, with the new Ministry of Munitions increasing the production of the largest ordnance from zero to 234 in three years. (J. & C. McCutcheon Collection)

Wounded British soldiers on a Red Cross train. Those in view in this picture look remarkably healthy, so perhaps they had 'Blighty' wounds – those considered serious enough for at least a spell back in the UK. Sending once-wounded soldiers back to the Front was commonplace. (J. & C. McCutcheon Collection)

Opposite bottom: Ambulance men line up in preparation for disembarking wounded soldiers who are unable to walk. Extra stretchers are lined up along the platform. (J. & C. McCutcheon Collection)

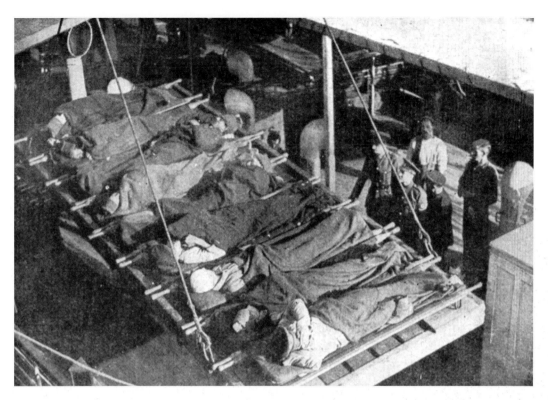

Above: Men who were unable to walk due to loss of their legs were hoisted off the hospital barges and put next to the waiting trains. (J. & C. McCutcheon Collection)

Left: Men on stretchers wait to be boarded. (J. & C. McCutcheon Collection)

Below: Men being carried from their train to the ambulances. (J. & C. McCutcheon Collection)

Inside a corridor ward on an ambulance train. Unfortunately, contemporary medicine could not deal with contaminated wounds, which often led to blood poisoning. (J. & C. McCutcheon Collection)

The London and South Western Railway loaned fifty locomotives to the War Office, thirty-six of them finding their way to France. This was a William Adams-designed 0-6-0 that 'did its bit' in the Middle East. (J. & C. McCutcheon Collection)

Railway Red Cross staff at work in an undergound passage at Waterloo station. These passages were used as hospitals during air raids. (J. & C. McCutcheon Collection)

Above: The 4th Royal Scots detraining at Edinburgh Waverley station. (J. & C. McCutcheon Collection)

Below: Former GNSR staff seen in the uniform of the Royal Army Medical Corps during the First World War. This branch of the Army was no sinecure or guarantee of protection from service on the front line. A recent study suggests that the work of stretcher-bearers, like these men, was the most harrowing and dangerous of the any experienced by men at war. (GNSRA)

Above: British troops return to London at the end of the war. (J. & C. McCutcheon Collection)

Opposite top: This LNWR locomotive, freshly named here as *Edith Cavell*, is shown decorated with flowers. The poster on the side of the locomotive says, 'Lest we forget.' (J. & C. McCutcheon Collection)

Opposite bottom: Proud members of the Royal Signals seen here were in fact employees of the Great North of Scotland Railway, and would hope to return to their old jobs one day. More than a quarter of British railwaymen were recruited in the First World War, either by voluntary enlistment or by conscription. (GNSRA)

Above: Artillery behind a Holt caterpillar tractor at Taunton station. (J. & C. McCutcheon Collection)

Opposite top: The walking wounded board No. 39, another hospital train, on 1 April 1918. (J. & C. McCutcheon Collection)

Opposite bottom: Royal Army Medical Corps staff attend to wounded soldiers being disembarked from an ambulance train on 27 April 1916. (J. & C. McCutcheon Collection)

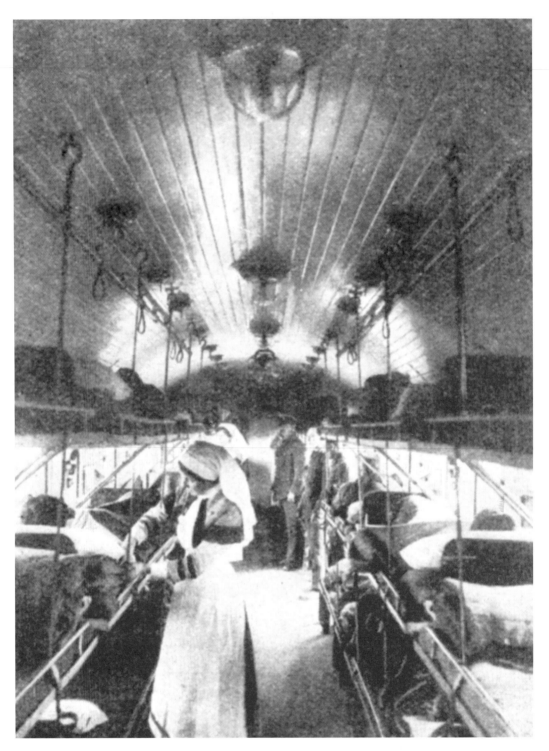

Another view inside a corridor ward on a ambulance train. This vehicle may have been pictured on the Continent, judging by the height available. Loading gauge became a crucial problem for ambulance trains in the UK, as they might have to operate anywhere on the network. Two of the railways with the most limited height profile were the Highland and the SE&CR – ironically, two of those most likely to convey wounded soldiers, either from the Continent or from northern fleet bases. (J. & C. McCutcheon Collection)

use the harbour for ammunition loading but a communications muddle meant that permission to build the 1,000-yard line in May 1915 was not received until the first munitions train was already on its way from the south! That it had only to wait ten days to reach the harbour must be something of a record in British railway construction.

***

As the war developed, there was one kind of passenger excursion whose existence had to be questioned. In Circular 375 the REC appeared to sanction the continued running of hunting specials, allowing the transport of supporters to hunts, and in some cases their horses. But the wording of the Circular on 9 September 1915 was entirely negative – 'the running of special trains should be discouraged', no cheap fares should be made available, 'and the conveyance of such passengers and horses should be cancelled'. With the companies 'free to decide' whether to continue this traffic, it was hardly the clearest of instructions. In any case, those young men who would be most likely to follow the hounds were already at the Front, where Siegfried Sassoon could only dream of his lost pastime. One senior officer, the Earl of Feversham, a director of the North Eastern, even took his deerhound with him to the Somme. It was their last hunt.

Making an ROD

To meet the increased logistical demand of maintaining and servicing what had turned into a standing army on the Continent, in April 1915 the War Office asked the REC to establish a unit which would operate beyond Britain's shores. Thus was born the Railway Operating Department (ROD), an essential unit for operating railways in British interests overseas, and one which might have been established some fifteen years earlier.

During the Boxer Rebellion in China, the British response was hampered by the locals' destruction of half of the railway mileage into what was then known as Peking (Beijing), thus impairing the movement of military reinforcements. It was soon revealed that the British Army had no more than forty engineers familiar with railway construction or operation, and considerable assistance had to be received from Russian sources.

But it took the opening of a conflict on a European scale to emphasise the necessity of good railway operations in military campaigns beyond Britain's shores. Historian Hamilton Ellis recorded an apparent transfer of French locomotives away from the area of the Front during what he called 'the first Great Retreat', presumably before the conflict stabilised at the Battle of the Marne. The observer he quotes was a nurse who witnessed 'an endless procession of engines running light in a westerly direction' and who later found 'scores of locomotives shunted and forgotten'. Whether true or not (and Ellis appears to have been something of a Francophobe), the time would come, in 1916, when the French would insist that their ally accept increased responsibility for transport.

Initially set up in two sections, mechanical and operational, the new department comprised three officers and 266 NCOs and sappers, all railway company volunteers. It was commanded by Cecil Paget, General Superintendent of the Midland, soon to be gazetted a Lieutenant-Colonel. After a brief visit to Longmoor for training, the new department's staff was sent straight to France, where the mechanical section began to examine and repair Belgian engines driven south to escape capture by the enemy. Meanwhile their operational colleagues began working new sidings at Boulogne, laid by the SECR, where that company's tank engines were in use for shunting purposes. A new, third, section, entirely staffed by L&NWR employees, was created in the following July, operating the main line between Hazebrouck and Poperinghe. Two more sections were also trained but their members were then returned to their companies for the time being.

By the end of 1916, the crying need in the ROD was for shunters – the human kind, those railway employees most at risk of accident. A total of 1,200 were required, even after members of clerical grades began retraining for the task, one they could scarcely have anticipated or relished taking up. Overall the ROD was short of no less than 17,500 men for its increased requirements, although it did succeed in reducing this to a shortfall of 2,500 by 1918, by effecting the transfer of men of 'B' medical standard from the Front Line. This success did not go unnoticed at Staff HQ, however, and during 1917, as Edwin Pratt reports, without comment, 'demand for men for the Fighting Units became so acute that drastic restrictions as to medical classification were placed on candidates for enlistment in the Railway Troops'. By the end of the war, the ROD comprised 24,000 men whose operations encompassed Russia and Egypt as well as France.

The locomotive most associated with the department was the Robinson 2-8-0 designed for the Great Central Railway three years before the war, and so associated, indeed, that it became known colloquially as the 'ROD 2-8-0'. Some 521 were supplied for overseas service, the first being delivered by North British Locomotive in August 1917 although only 305 actually operated overseas, and only six were produced at the Great Central's own works. By this later stage of the war, the railway companies appeared to occupy the end of the queue for metal supply, particularly copper, necessary for firebox construction, but equally vital for armament production. All the ROD 2-8-0s were offered on loan to domestic railways after the war, 152 being used by the L&NWR, ninety-three by the GCR itself, seventy-six by the GWR, fifty by the Caledonian, and forty-four by the GER, in addition to smaller amounts. Many were sold to home railways – thirty to the L&NWR, 105 to the LMS, 100 to the GWR and 273 to the LNER. Some were sold overseas, the unit price sinking as low as £340 in the mid-1920s, and some disposed of overseas. Sadly, while all those sent abroad survived the First World War, when ninety-seven were moved to the Middle East in the next conflict, none returned.

The Railways Commanded II

As previously mentioned, accountants from six companies met five days after the August 1914 ultimatum to discuss the financial relationship between the REC and the railways it co-ordinated. Even then, it was realised that future dealings between Whitehall and the company boardrooms would have to allow for more than just the hiring of a troop train to move the BEF to Southampton, or transport materials into Woolwich Arsenal, and ammunition out of there to the nearest port. Far-sightedly, it was recorded that, if the railways were to service the many-faceted needs of the military, 'at the end of the period of control, the companies might submit a claim for such [large] amount as they would require to spend on arrears, in order to bring lines and rolling-stock up to normal conditions'. This would appear to represent common sense, but it was not until August 1915 that the Treasury agreed that payments to railways (which had started at the beginning of that year) would address 'arrears of repair and renewal of rolling-stock, plus a percentage to cover the increased outlay' anticipated later. Pratt reported that this was designed to avoid the railways presenting Government with a 'repair bill', as it were, 'of so large a figure … that much friction between the Government and themselves might result'. By this time, he added drily, it was already obvious that the war was going on longer than originally expected.

Nevertheless, the REC, in its provisional planning, still paid lip service to the idea of a short sharp war. In Circular 330 the companies were told that statistics for business returns need not be submitted quarterly, but could be allowed to run to the end of that year, or 'to the close of the Control period in the event of it terminating before the end of 1915'. This was evidence of a good relationship between Government and the nation's railways, spoiled somewhat by comments from the Government auditor midway through that year asking for details on how some company figures for the first war period, to the end of 1914, had been arrived at, particular in areas of 'pool balances and disputed demurrage'. (This problem is explained below.) The committee asked the companies to satisfy the auditor directly, if they had not already provided the information. In fact subventions had been paid very promptly in the first six weeks of 1915, as company archives confirm. The companies had already been assured by the REC, as early as October 1914, that the Income Tax Commissioners could be informed that the tax payments for that autumn were being deferred while the subvention details were finalised. Whether the commissioners had actually agreed to this was not exactly clear!

* * *

By November of the following year, there was a further redefining of what payments would be made to the railways, and how this would be done. The running of troop trains and other requested workings would be paid for through the REC by effectively guaranteeing that there would be no loss of net profit, taking 1913 as the relevant example, and not through accounting for individual operations. But the need for clarity in accounting was obvious, and was itemised once and for all in November 1916. The quarterly payments to keep up net profit levels would cover everything except the following services, which the Admiralty, War Office, or Ministry of Munitions would have to settle directly with the contracted railway company. These comprised:

Special services.
Season tickets.
Transport for dockyard officials.
Occupation of railway property.
Supply of water, gas, and electricity (where the railway was using contracted supplies rather than supplying from its own resources).
Repairs to HM ships from railway works (but not applying to railway-owned vessels).
Servicemen travelling 'on police warrants'.
Any other services.

The transport of carrier pigeons was classed as too important to include in the above miscellany, and ranked along with the chartering of troop trains, accounted for centrally. In May 1916 it was decided to change the name 'War Office Pigeon Service' to 'Home Forces Pigeon Service', the former acronym perhaps being thought disrespectful to any Italian visitor to Britain who might become aware of it. REC Circular 572 did, however, permit the use of labels printed with 'W.O.P.S.' to continue to be used until stocks were exhausted.

* * *

'Disputed demurrage' was mentioned earlier as a possible complication in finalising a railway company's receipts, and the Government auditor was justified in discerning a problem here. First, a definition: Demurrage is, according to the OED, a 'delay, hesitation, or detention'. It is recorded as having first been used in a textbook of railway legislation in 1858, and in this context means the time during which a wagon was unloaded at its destination, and unavailable for further commercial use. A wagon owned by the railway (as opposed to a private-owner vehicle) could remain on a customer's siding for up to forty-eight hours while awaiting or undergoing unloading. After that there was a 'rental' fee of 1s 6d per day for the average-sized truck, but 10s for one of more than 30 tons' capacity.

Unfortunately, in the first autumn of the war it became obvious that there was an increase in the number of rail vehicles being literally sidelined in commercial and industrial premises, with one railway company reporting an increase of 160 per cent in overdue fees being incurred. Upon investigating, the REC found that some customer firms were prepared to pay, or at least concede, the charges, with one company being threatened by legal action in the following spring, for owing nearly £6,000. When the committee enquired why there should be any delay in returning rail vehicles to traffic at such a busy time, it was explained that commercial firms were experiencing a serious shortage of muscle power – both human and equine – to undertake unloading, as well as a reduction of storage space at a time of high productivity.

Even a Government body such as the Ministry of Munitions was experiencing similar difficulties, with the discovery that one ROF in Scotland had no fewer than 560 wagons awaiting attention, with only enough labour available to unload seventy per day. This was uncovered by a committee hurriedly set up in September 1915, by the REC appointing superintendents from each of the companies on the managing committee. Their remit was to undertake a roving role in investigating traffic problems and, where possible, easing bottlenecks in the network. As well as meeting at the Railway Clearing House every Tuesday until May 1916, these troubleshooters, as they might be called in modern parlance, took their roving commission literally. At Carlisle they discovered another 800 wagons awaiting movement on to the Scottish ROF mentioned earlier (and almost certainly Gretna), and helped loosen the logjam. They also assisted with 'certain difficulties' with the transmission of Admiralty coal in its marathon journey northwards from South Wales, and helped sort out a problem with the movement of 'rough (unsorted) empties' on the L&SWR main line. The idea of a railway traffic 'flying squad' was a good one and its disbandment after the summer of 1916 a little surprising.

* * *

Increased holiday traffic was hardly what the companies had anticipated as the war went on, at least until 1917. The REC's 'business as usual' policy encouraged the public to *expect* their usual holidays in wartime, and when women's wages began to augment the average family's spending power, the railways found themselves with increased holiday traffic even as the British Army flung itself against the German wire on the Somme in the summer of 1916. Excursion traffic was booming in Britain; ordinary people had never had it so good, with many families having their womenfolk earning good wages in munitions, light engineering, and clerical jobs normally held by men. Blackpool landladies were reportedly amazed at the increased demand for accommodation, while on Saturday 29 July 1916, the Cornish Riviera Express carried no fewer than 2,027 passengers in three sections to holiday destinations in the West Country.

While this hedonism might appear shocking – civilians enjoying themselves while ignoring the hardships and privations of the fighting men over the Channel – it should be borne in mind that the newspapers fed the public a constant diet of optimism, misinformation, and downright lies about how well the war was going. In February 1915 Lloyd George had complained of 'the Press treating the progress of the war as one of almost unbroken success'. No wonder the British public believed that a good time could be had by all.

Even a 50 per cent increase in fares in 1917 failed to stem the demand for what the authorities might well define as 'unnecessary' travel, and in particular omitted season tickets which may have been too low anyway, where companies had been attempting to build up commuter traffic over the years in areas where they owned land approved for housing. In addition to this, there were huge demands to be made on the network in the form of troop specials, and entirely new freight traffic streams, while some companies were supplying locomotives and rolling stock to neighbour companies, or to the armed forces themselves, even before 1917. Because of this failure in long-term planning, greater strictures had to be introduced in that year, with no fewer than 400 passenger stations closed until the war was over (as will be discussed). Not surprisingly, historian James Hamilton described 'business as usual' as 'surely the most senseless slogan ever to be coined for a nation engaged in a major war'.

It was not long before the REC and the Ministry of Munitions looked to the canal system to assist the railways.

In for the Duration

Railway Canals

If British canals are nowadays regarded as placid backwaters enhancing the landscape, there was surprisingly little difference in 1914. Inland waterways were already taking on the appearance of dereliction and underuse, so much so that a royal commission was created in 1906 to consider their future. Three years later, its published report stopped short of blaming railways for the canals' plight – although some of the evidence heard was fairly damaging – but recommended nationalisation.

More than one-third of canal mileage was owned or managed by railway companies, usually as a result of the original operators meeting defeat at the hands of a newer form of transport technology. Thus, such well-known waterways as the Birmingham Navigations, Trent & Mersey, and Kennet & Avon, came under the suzerainty of railway companies from the 1840s onwards. Even such supposedly independent waterways as the Sheffield & South Yorkshire and the Leeds & Liverpool were effectively influenced or even controlled, either through rail ownership of major shareholdings, as in the former example, or the leasing of toll rights, as in the latter.

Railway management of so many waterways continued in some cases after Nationalisation in 1948, while even today (2014), there is still one canal owned by Network Rail (the Stover in Devon, although it plays no further part in this narrative). Railway companies could hardly be expected to invest in their canals which were, after all, failed business competitors. However, the waterways' statutory origin guaranteed rights of navigation which required an Order in parliament to nullify; action which could be challenged by any local authority or other interested party, and likely to prove expensive. Cheaper just to leave the canals as they were, bringing in some income through water supply to industry, revenue which could be gleaned without expensive lock maintenance.

* * *

While railway canals were (theoretically at least) under Government control from the REC in 1914, the remainder began the war in a form of administrative limbo. It certainly appeared that if any transport network required an overall supervisory body armed with a budget to finance technical improvements in 1914, it was the British canal system – especially considering the chronic problem posed by the narrower locks of the Black Country. The increasing demands of a conflict rapidly turning into a war of attrition meant that Britain's internal transport facilities would be at full stretch for the foreseeable future. It must have been obvious that an overall organisation representing the waterways was by now becoming a necessity; one which the Board of Trade belatedly attempted to address. Acting REC Chairman Sir Herbert Walker concluded in a letter in December 1916, regarding ammunition transport to France, that he hoped that the Ministry of Munitions would take up the matter with the canal companies. Within a fortnight, a senior Ministry official had organised a meeting of canal owners and carriers to ensure that the urgency of the challenge was made clear to them, but, in turn, was soon acquainted with the greatest immediate problem faced by the canals – lack of manpower.

As on the railways, the outbreak of the First World War triggered an immediate loss of experienced men; by the spring of 1917, the shortfall was so bad as to require Government intervention twice-over – in restricting military recruitment from among remaining boatmen, and in assigning units of the new transport battalions. These were formed in 1916, originally to undertake work in the nations' docks, but directed to carry out no less than 126,679 days work on canals in the following year, with the L&NWR-controlled Birmingham network taking up approximately one-third of these.

* * *

Not until 1917 was a department of the board focussed on the supervision of the remaining 1,390 miles of Britain's waterways that became known as 'controlled' canals. These were not owned by the railways, but operated under the aegis of the Canal Control Committee (of the Board of Trade). Its history need not concern us in this book, except to point out that each of its three regional committees included a representative of a major railway, and this excelled the arrangements for the Docks & Inland Waterways Executive specifically set up 1948 to make such a liaison. Considerably so; each of three British CCC sub-committees also included a railway representative – Southern (covering 320 miles, with GWR liaison), Midland (658 miles, L&NWR), North (412 miles, Lancashire & Yorkshire) – of Great Britain, and (later) one for Irish waterways. The presence of railway representation was a practical concession to reality, given the need for transport co-ordination at a time of war.

In attempting to further the work of the committees, CCC staff circulated letters to all Chambers of Commerce to encourage their members to avail themselves of canal transport wherever and whenever possible, and historian Edwin Pratt goes so far as to suggest that the committee members 'got into *personal* communication with local traders' in an effort to persuade them to transfer from rail to canal. (This author's italics.) But a more formal initiative was the CCC's decision to produce a handbook to the waterways 'issued [through His Majesty's Stationery Office] to afford information to senders and receivers of goods and materials ... to enable them to use the inland waterways of the country to the utmost extent'. Priced sixpence, this ran into a second edition and provided contact information and maps of the canal system – everything a manufacturer or supplier might need to facilitate a decision on transport methods. It seems a curious idea, namely a government department publishing a catalogue of commercial services available to other unrestricted private businesses, and a better example of the compromised attitude of the times to transport nationalisation would be hard to find. Incidentally, a number of waterways were shown on the *Handbook*'s map – for example, the Basingstoke, Derby, Ulverston, and Witham – but were not mentioned as transport options in the text of the book (significantly perhaps, the latter two were railway-controlled).

The Government's determination to divert traffic to the canals stood in contrast to the intentional routing of port-to-port transport within the UK by discriminatory pricing – but not by canal. To ensure the safety of a consignment of, for example, sugar, requiring transport from Liverpool to Bristol, when the U-boat danger was at its height, the railway was subsidised so as to make the shipping alternative uneconomic – at 16*s* 6*d* per ton by rail as opposed to 23*s* 9*d* by ship. But the point was missed that both these ports were connected by internal waterway and that bulk cargoes – in this case, in 10 ton consignments – could have been conveyed by canal boat. Admittedly, this would require the use of narrow boats, whether either the Shropshire Union or Trent & Mersey was used, but the equivalent of five such loads could have been conveyed in a single pairing of boat and 'butty' if the transport authorities had seen canals as a serious alternative to the railway. Instead, here was a case of railways being specified for internal cargoes, even if the network was busy enough already. In contrast, the public was being discouraged from using railways at this time, certainly from January 1917, with a fares increase and reduction in services.

What had prompted a governmental decision to place an authoritative body over the independently owned canals was the massive loss of waterway traffic at a time when the railways were overloaded. Between 1913 and 1916 the Aire & Calder showed a 40 per cent drop in tonnage carried, and the Grand Junction, 24 per cent. This was primarily because of a lack of boatmen. Under control conditions the overall decline slowed to around 15 per cent comparing the Augusts of 1916 and 1917, although the decline steepened slightly in the following year. Nevertheless, this first experience of state authoritarianism may be considered a partial success, particularly as the board authorised £3 million worth of subsidies during the control period. Even Edwin Pratt – no enthusiast for state control, and whose statistics are quoted above – conceded that 'the decline [in tonnage carried] would doubtless have been considerably greater but for the control'.

Probably the most positive aspect of the CCC's work was the attention paid to manpower problems on the waterways. In March 1917 it was discovered that no fewer than 1,200 boats were lying idle because of a lack of crews, due to military recruiting, whether for volunteers or conscripts. As a result, from the following month, 'Protection cards' were issued to canal workers over the age of twenty-five to prevent their being called up by the military, 'unless the holder discontinued working on the canals or was continually unsatisfactory in regard to that work'. In June it was decided to build on this decision by drafting in labour from the Transport Workers' Battalions. These had been established in March 1916 to counter the decline in the number of dockers and stevedores available to work Britain's ports, but their tasks were extended within thirteen months to include railway loading and unloading where necessary, and waterways working by June 1917. All this reflected the lack of mechanisation in docks and goods depots almost everywhere, while offering tacit criticism of the 'take 'em all' attitude to military recruiting.

* * *

To counter the lack of experienced boatmen, the Southern Committee very enterprisingly set up a training school for battalion personnel in 1917. This was done with the cooperation of the Great Western Railway, using one of its handily little-used waterways, namely the Kennet & Avon. Located at Devizes, the school trained some 200 men in groups of thirty over a three-week course, including tuition on loading and unloading, and working with horses and locks. (With a 'flight' of twenty-nine locks nearby, its central section later described by Tom Rolt as 'the most spectacular in England', Devizes was an ideal location for tuition in working the last-named aspect of canals.) Pratt records curiously that the school closed when the canal companies 'found that men really could be trained to work on the canals without having been actually born and bred thereon', and undertook their own training. Again, the intervention of government could hardly have been seen in a more positive light.

Interestingly, in all the attention given by the CCC to the manpower problem in the First World War, no consideration seems to have been given to drafting in *women* power. This certainly happened in the next war, and, although women were to be found working on the railways and on municipal transport networks in the First World War, canals seem to have been seen as a task too far for 'drafted' women workers in the first world conflict.

The CCC represented a belated attempt to relieve pressure on the railway system in wartime, but such pressure was arguably the result of a failure on the behalf of the then new REC in the first place, in permitting a 'business as usual' approach from the start. A major example of the railways' predominance of the nation's canals in time of war, but before the central administration of non-railway canals was addressed by Government, can be seen in a letter, briefly referred to earlier, written by Sir Herbert Walker on 7 December 1916. Walker told the Secretary of the Ministry of Munitions that 'We think the time has come when the Ministry of Munitions should take in hand the question of the better use of canals throughout the country for the transport of raw materials used in the manufacture of munitions of war'. In particular, Walker proposed that it should be possible to transport ordnance from the 'filling factories', where shell and bullet casings were filled, to coastal ports, to be met by sea-going barges 'capable of negotiating the canals in France [but] it will not be possible for the self-same barges to work over the canals in this country'. The military was already thinking along these lines, and was looking to minimise the trans-shipment process.

The military authorities were given exclusive use of the Folkestone–Boulogne passage, barred to civilian traffic from 29 November 1915, but even this prioritisation was insufficient to meet the military's needs for cross-Channel shipping. It was decided to create a new port to handle war *matériel*, and they settled on the Kent coast at Richborough, near Sandwich. Even although not fully functional until early 1917, this new port was to make a telling contribution to the logistics of supplying a permanent British Army on the continent. Significantly, the port came to be associated with two transport innovations. One was train ferries, already common overseas, but rarely used in Britain since the mid-nineteenth century. The second introduction was that of continental-style barges, and this echoed Walker's call.

It was decided that, instead of loading and unloading ships, which required deeper berths and were easily detected by submarines when in open water, seagoing barges would provide a better means of transporting *matériel* over a comparatively short seaway. They would of course also have the advantage of being able to penetrate the continental canal system, thus reaching inland depots supplying the armed services. Ideally, they should also be able to operate in the English canal network too, but with some of the later craft having loading capacities of 1,000 tons – there were fifteen available by March 1919 – this was obviously out of the question. But at least half of this transport solution could be achieved through transporting ammunition etc. by rail to Richborough, loading there into barges, and taking it across the Channel to ports inland.

The success of the initiative to construct an entirely new port can be surmised from the statistics. In twenty-two months, no less than 1.28 million tons of material, mostly ammunition, were despatched to the Continent in barges, nearly 1 million tons of which were taken to internal canal depots. This was in addition to rail cargoes, so it is surprising to see Kentish railway author, Patrick Ransome-Wallis, dismiss Richborough as a wartime white elephant. This was all part of a cross-Channel operation to move such everyday supplies as food, nearly all of which had to be transported to a British port by rail. By 10 November 1918, 25.5 million tons of stores had been supplied to British forces on the Western Front, approximately one-eighth comprising foodstuffs, although this statistic was exceeded by horse fodder at 5.3 million tons. 'Railway materials' – presumably for the use of ROD personnel – stood at just short of 1 million tons. Richborough was also used in the Second World War for the assembly of Mulberry floating harbours, making possible the greatest opposed landing in history.

Unfortunately, British canals proved largely unable to adapt to the transport needs of a nation fighting a total war. If Britain had boasted a more versatile waterways system – and who is to say that railways were instrumental in preventing that – Richborough might not have been necessary. Taking the long view, it could be said that in 1916 canals failed the first challenge of a new, increasingly violent, century.

It is worth considering the words of the official historian C. I. Savage, writing after the Second World War, during which canals once again failed to offer railways relief from traffic pressure at a time of crisis: 'The value of canals in the war of 1914–18 had been comparatively small and … instead of being a second means of inland transport, they had become a bad third.'

More Manpower

Within six months of the outbreak of war, recruiting became a spectre which would haunt British society, and not least, the railways. Lord Kitchener, Minister of War, had quickly grasped the fact that victory would not be achieved by galloping cavalry – even if some of his generals still longed for such a prospect – but would require vast numbers of infantrymen. Not surprisingly, the railway companies, many of them huge commercial concerns and all of them labour-intensive, represented apparently brimming reservoirs of manpower – nearly two-thirds of a million men.

The REC's Circular number 61 had been a reasonable document to advise railway companies on recruitment matters, conceding the right of the individual to offer his services to the colours, but simultaneously affording his employer the opportunity to point out, to any recruiting officer, the man's usefulness to the British transport network, which was dedicated to satisfying the armed services' traffic demands. By 1 March 1915, 6,720 staff requests for release had been refused by the railways, leaving the railwayman concerned with the sole option of resignation if he wished to enlist. Such a commitment by the individual would have to precede the now unemployed man facing an inevitable medical examination, although there was little chance of *that* being a bar to recruitment, one suspects.

But Kitchener would not be deterred, and on 4 March, Walker was obliged to circulate, in Circular (or, more aptly, 'Instruction') 215 a request for the railway companies to provide the REC with details of male staff in three age grades (under eighteen, eighteen–forty, and over forty) who might be suitable for military service. Significantly, this missive was headed 'Private and Confidential'. Despite Circular 61, this should not have come as a surprise to the acting chairman; in number 141 he had commented on an initiative by the Parliamentary Recruiting Committee to conduct a census of men, between nineteen and thirty-eight, 'willing to enlist for the War only' [i.e. the duration]. This was to be done through leafleting householders, and Walker urged railway staff, if lodging, to declare to their landlords that they would require to request employers' permission to enlist.

Railways large and small were of course major householders themselves in 1915, from the Cockermouth, Keswick & Penrith Railway's stock of twenty-eight houses, and the Cambrian with fifty-one, through the Midland's 5,108, to the largest houseowner, the L&NWR, with 9,003. Walker's circular could be viewed as an instruction to the railways to collect the information themselves, but the REC acting chairman was not passing on orders slavishly.

Herbert Walker was prepared to fight his, and the railways', corner against any unreasonable demand of the encroaching 'Total War'. He requested, and was granted, an interview with Kitchener at this time, and the latter accepted that the railways could not be expected to supply staff indiscriminately. But concessions had to be made, the first being the withdrawal of 1,869 objections to the recruitment of railway staff. Walker agreed that the railways would establish what proportion of their staffs were indispensable, as compared to those whose work could be undertaken by youths under the age of eighteen, by women, or by changed working practices. A sub-committee was immediately established to investigate this, chaired by Frank Potter, general manager of the Great Western. In some spirit of reconciliation, in mid-June 1915, the Board of Trade authorised a badge for staff, with words 'RAILWAY SERVICE' and the company's name prominent, to protect the wearer from the heartless donation of white feathers. But 20,000 additional railwaymen joined the armed services in that summer alone.

Still more were needed. After the failure of a recruitment initiative in 1915 headed by Lord Derby, conscription was coming. The Military Service Act passed on 5 January 1916 effectively drafted every unmarried male in the nation aged between eighteen and forty-one, with those who believed themselves ineligible having to argue their case before a regional tribunal. Effective from 2 March that year, it is significant that only a few thousand railwaymen were found to be either 'unattested' through Derby's scheme, or disqualified through a previous objection by their company employer. More conscriptive legislation followed in May of that year, and by October the top twelve railway companies had lost more than 40 per cent of their pre-war staff either to the forces, or to munitions factories located on railway premises.

By April 1917, the Government's official statistical digest lists nearly ¼ million railwaymen occupying a 'reserved occupation' – a new term, it appears – the total being over 400,000 if other transport workers were included, and representing around 15 per cent of all those listed as exempt from call-up. By 1918, so desperate was the Army for new men that even munition workers could expect to be drafted. (100,000 'skilled and semi-skilled' in the twelve months up to April, according to figures given to parliament by the then minister, Winston Churchill.) By that time, not only were railway staff being shipped to France, they were taking much of their railway infrastructure with them, as will be related in due course.

Accidents

In the *Railway Yearbook* for 1916 there is a list of accidents for the previous year on Britain's railways. By far the most disastrous of these was Quintinshill on 22 May 1915, but that year saw four other incidents, accounting for an additional twenty-seven lives and making 1915 a bad year for accidents even without the carnage near Gretna when 227 men were killed. In contrast, there had been six passenger deaths on Britain's railways in 1914 and would be only three in 1916. Similarly there was a rise in the number of injuries in the centre of triennial 1914–16, namely 322, 1,432, and 350, respectively. The statistics for the war up until the end of 1918 comprised 114 passenger fatalities if the Quintinshill figure is removed. In contrast, a similar sample period in the previous decade reveals 133 deaths, so one might interpret this as a gradual – and perhaps *too* gradual – improvement in rail travel safety. But it is impossible to ignore that one toll from 22 May 1915 – it was, arguably, a direct result of staff working under pressure, although other factors were present, as will be discussed.

There were five fatal accidents in the year 1915, two of them on the L&NWR and one of these involving the 'Irish Mail'. A derailment following mechanical failure was the cause of eight deaths at Weedon, while there was a solitary casualty in a lesser accident at Bletchley. The Great Eastern had the misfortune of a death on New Year's Day, following a misreading of signals, but there were seventeen deaths in County Durham after a double collision. In one sense this accident was *worse* than Quintinshill in that it resembled it, yet no lessons had been learned from the disaster in Dumfriesshire.

* * *

War demands had increased traffic on the West Coast Main Line in May 1915, and on the morning of the 22nd, the loops were full on both sides of the line at Quintinshill, the first signal box in Scotland passed by northbound trains. This caused a problem for the signal staff when the early morning all-stations 'Parliamentary' arrived, as it would delay the overnight service from Euston running late behind. The signalman coming to the end of his shift that morning decided to move the 'local' from the 'down' (northbound) line to the 'up', thus clearing the way for the express. The locomotive fireman came into the box to confirm that his train was now stopped in section, but the signalman failed to place a safeguard on the relevant signal lever, which was correctly at danger. Almost immediately, a troop train from the north was offered by the next signal box, but the signalman was now being relieved by his daytime colleague, who had arrived late (on the local train) and was busy falsifying paperwork to cover this up. The latter accepted the train, despite the existence of the 'local' standing only a few feet away. A collision was now inevitable, the double-headed southbound troop special racing towards the stationary train at some 60 mph. While this was terrible enough, the northbound overnight train ran into the wreckage immediately afterwards. To make matters worse, the troop special was composed largely of older Great Central stock, lit by gas, which now leaked under pressure, was ignited by locomotive coals, and caught fire.

This awful accident at Quintinshill could probably have been averted if track circuiting had been fitted. True, this was not the opinion of the Board of Trade inspector who conducted the subsequent inquiry, although his justification for the non-installation of this simple and inexpensive system scarcely stands up to examination. He opined that the view from the signal box was good in both directions, when in fact this was not equally true for locomotive crews whose sightlines were obscured by a bend to the north (as signalling expert and railway author O. S. Nock later discovered on a footplate trip); in any event, the loss of visibility at night or in mist surely invalidated the inspector's comment. As early as 1880, an official reporting on an accident at Nine Elms had suggested that track circuiting would have prevented it happening. Indeed the Board of Trade inspector examining an accident uncannily similar, although mercifully less catastrophic, than Quintinshill, later in 1915 in County Durham, might well have recommended the installation of track circuiting. Many years later, in 1952, a chief inspector of railways remarked that one formal accident inquiry in every ten would have been rendered unnecessary if track circuiting had been in widespread operation – one suspects this is a conservative estimate.

In the *Railway Yearbook* for 1916, the accident figures are given on page 37, with the Quintinshill figure prominent. Twelve pages earlier there is a list of companies utilising such technical features as track circuiting, and the Caledonian Railway appeared to have equipped only one site, in the city of Glasgow. Opposite that list, was an advertisement for the engineering firm of McKenzie, Holland & Westinghouse, offering 'AC and DC track circuiting and electric lever locking for train protection'. Such a fitting would very probably have prevented the Quintinshill signal crews from 'forgetting' the local train standing on the wrong running line. But because of their apparent complacency the railwaymen found themselves in the dock of the High Court of the Justiciary.

Why were the directors not also prosecuted for failing to install a readily available safety device to protect their customers? One modern historian has suggested that electrical signalling could not have been installed at any rural location at this time as there was no 'national grid', but the company could have generated its own power. The current required need not be much more than 100 volts, the amount of conducting materials would be negligible – as the rail would be the conductor – and the power could have been produced relatively cheaply over a considerable length of line, using a stationary steam engine in a small power plant.

Two of the three railwaymen involved at the Scottish accident were convicted and imprisoned, one for three years of penal servitude. The line was not track-circuited by the Caledonian afterwards, or by subsequent owners the LMS, or BR at first, and not completely for another fifty-five years.

* * *

In the final two years of war there were four accidents on Britain's railways involving munitions cargoes. It was a miracle that there were no fatalities, and in particular, no explosions. But with a mushrooming munitions industry producing its deadly products in ever-increasing numbers, the railways found themselves having to transport material between factories – artillery shells and their contents were not usually produced on the same site – and then moving the finished ordnance to a port.

More planning might have been expected, but the railways appear to have lost sight of the immediate problem. Railway steamers could only transport explosives in small amounts on passenger vessels (and this was not a good idea in itself), but it certainly seems that crossed fingers were the principal means of ensuring safety on Britain's main lines. The use of open wagons for munitions transport was clearly inadvisable and indicated that there were simply not enough 'Gunpowder' vans, as they were called, to provide covered transport. The lack of safety equipment – even something as basic as a water supply – does not appear to have concerned anyone. It was mercifully fortuitous that only once was a passenger train involved in collision with a munitions working, but perhaps the authorities could have used their newfound powers to limit passenger services on routes frequented by munitions traffic. (There was at least one such example, on the Highland system.) In an age of overweening control, there was not enough when it came to explosives transport.

Feeding the hungry guns in France would seem likely to involve the London Brighton & South Coast Railway, but when an accident happened on the London–Brighton main line in 1918, explosives were being carried in both directions. This accident occurred near Redhill, when a London-bound goods train came to a stop in Redstone tunnel on 18 April. The train had split in two, and before a following goods working could be stopped, it rammed the stationary rear section of the divided train. Derailed wagons were now fouling the down line, and were hit by a southbound train, creating a trail of debris 40 feet long and as high as the tunnel ceiling. Incredibly, nobody was hurt, but *all three* trains were carrying ammunition. Led by George Andrews, foreman at the company's carriage and wagon depot at New Cross, staff managed to carefully extricate the cargo over a period of three days, a feat of courage which is almost unimaginable as the deadly material was removed by hand and carried to safety, with an explosion a possibility at any time. Mr Andrews was awarded the OBE for his courage, but everyone risking their lives must have been similarly deserving.

This was the second accident on the LBSCR in a matter of months, and it has to be said that nothing had been learned from the previous incident involving explosives. A goods train had caught fire near a town in the south of England (as described even after the war), on 22 September 1917, when three open wagons containing ammunition began burning. An intrepid inspector, Charles Carne, found (with difficulty) a supply of water and clambered aboard the vehicles, not ceasing his efforts until he had doused the flames and secured the site. Deservedly, he was awarded the Albert Medal by King George V. But no special precautions seem to have been taken to protect such a delicate cargo, nor were there measures immediately available to deal with a possible fire.

Unfortunately there were other incidents involving the transport of munitions. A goods train became derailed near Paisley on 11 September 1916, and its wagons, including three conveying gunpowder in nitro-cellulose, fouled a nearby running line. Predictably, a passenger train immediately hit the derailed vehicles, but by a miracle nobody was badly hurt and there was no explosion. Within three weeks, the same company (the Caledonian) experienced another accident when a goods train split in two on a downward gradient. The second half collided with the first, derailing nineteen wagons. Three of them were loaded with cordite. Again, fortune favoured the careless, and there was no explosion, and no injuries.

An unusual instance of ammunition being carried in a passenger train came about in March 1918, when the German army, refreshed with troops from victory on the Eastern Front, smashed its way towards the Channel coast. The 12.20 lunchtime train from London (Victoria) to Folkestone was reserved for staff officers, but during the crisis three vans were attached daily, loaded with small arms ammunition. At Folkestone this was taken to a nearby airfield for flying across to France (although three railway vans could carry rather more than a planeload), and the bullets were probably being fired even before nightfall.

Perhaps not all was fully professional in the munitions industry, either, when it came to safety matters. Edwin Pratt reported on the 'indiscriminate loading of gunpowder [vans] and other special vehicles at Woolwich Arsenal, where this work was entirely in the hands of the government authorities and beyond the control of the SECR'. Considering how regimented transport had become at the time, and the Government's takeover of the munitions industry, the lack of precautionary care in the loading and transporting of explosives and their constituents was surprising, to say the least.

* * *

Even without outright accidents, involving collisions or derailments, railway work could be as unpleasant as any, and probably more dangerous than most. The most hazardous task on the railways was that of the shunters. With nearly all British goods wagons fitted with only a handbrake, it was necessary to have shunters working in every goods yard, walking or running alongside trains dropping off or collecting vehicles. A hooked pole was used to lift the three-link coupling to accomplish this, but a missed footing could easily result in serious injury, or worse. As it was, thirty-four shunters died in 1913, one for every 441 employed. Permanent way men were the next most likely to be killed, statistically speaking, on Britain's railways that year – 1 in 618 – while the safest were what were classified 'miscellaneous labourers', who might very well be working away from the tracks, at one death for every 3,361. Engine drivers were slightly more likely to die at work than their firemen. Accident accounts often showed a driver encouraging his mate to 'jump' if a collision seemed inevitable. (Not that this was any guarantee of salvation.) Curiously there was a 50 per cent increase in footplate fatalities between 1910 and the outbreak of war.

At the height of war, there were 414 deaths among railway employees (including a small number of contractors) and 3,701 injured, all this in the year 1916 alone. Increase in traffic and the introduction of some 'blackout' conditions in eastern areas may account for these alarming figures, and there were forty-four deaths among shunters, who might be directly affected by these factors. (In theory, a change to DORA in 1917 gave railways exemption from lighting restrictions.) Permanent Way workers were the most vulnerable in 1916, with no fewer than eighty-nine killed and 125 injured, and works mechanics and goods guards were also vulnerable, with twenty-five deaths in both categories. Drivers in this year seemed to survive more than firemen, at seventeen fatalities to twenty-one.

Suffice to say that soldiering may have seemed an attractive alternative to working on the railway, with its chronic potential for accidents. And it was into this cauldron that women were to be thrown in unprecedented numbers.

Female Workers

Women were already being employed on Britain's railways before 1914. They were to be found mainly in clerical grades, the L&NWR being the largest employer at the outbreak of war, with 2,123 employed, just over 2 per cent of the company workforce. The North Eastern was next with 1,470, followed by the Midland's 1,396, and the Great Western's 1,371. In terms of wartime recruitment, the L&NWR also led with ultimate figures of 9,154, the Midland being next, with 9,000. The North Eastern followed with 7,885 and the Great Western with 6,345. But the staff shortfall was still considerable, as shown in the table below.

Staff Shortfall on Britain's Railways in the First World War
(Four largest in order of total female recruitment)

	Men out	Women 1914	Women in	Total women
L&NWR	31,742	2,123	7,031	9,154
Midland	21,813	1,396	7,604	9,000
North Eastern	18,339	1,470	6,385	7,885
Great Western	25,479	1,371	4,974	6,345

Totals shown in the first and third columns are not direct comparisons from any particular date, although they indicate the extent of the employment shortfall. NER figures exclude around 1,000 women recruited to the National Projectile Factory on company ground at Darlington.

In a recent review of women's work in the First World War, journalist Kate Adie points out that the railways were paying barely half a man's wage for a woman to do the same job, although the official version was that women were paid on the bottom rate of pay which the post carried. Nevertheless, the average station porter was paid 53*s* a week if male, but 10*s* less if female. Male ticket collectors were paid 64*s* 5*d* per week, and female, 46*s*. The biggest discrepancy in weekly pay was, perhaps surprisingly, to be found in clerical work, where a man earned 83*s*, more than twice what a woman would take home, yet women might very well already have typing skills.

All this is evidence that companies were not losing financially in the labour market, particularly since women's service was well regarded. And there was no shortage of recruits when the railways opened their operational grades to women in the spring of 1915. This followed negotiations between the REC and the unions, principally the National Union of Railwaymen, whose constitution did not exclude women members, and there was a majority in favour of female membership by the summer of 1915, although they were not accorded full union rights. The timing was fortuitous for railway managements – once Lloyd George's creation, the Ministry of Munitions, became fully operational in 1916, no transport concern would be able to offer anything like the wages available in the arms factories. Weekly earnings of £10 were not unknown, and younger women were quite prepared to leave home to take up jobs in the large arsenals outside existing cities. Also, there was a limit to what railway work could be undertaken by women, since so much 'on the lines' was learned over years, and there was little of what we would now call 'in-service training'.

* * *

The total number of women working on the railways in the war years is believed to have totalled around 100,000, with some 65,887 employed in 1918. This works out at one woman for every three male vacancies, although there was a retraction in services, and indeed the actual network, from January 1917. As for safety issues, it must be said that the fatalities statistics of twenty-four female deaths between 1915 and 1920 seems remarkably low. Of course, women served in only one of the four most dangerous jobs – in order of increasing danger, permanent way worker, fireman, driver, and shunter – with a number taking part in the first of these categories. But the nature of the accidents described by Helena Wojtczak, in her authoritative book *Railwaywomen*, will leave the reader in no doubt that women shared the daily dangers facing transport staff at a time of lighting restrictions and an enemy attacking Great Britain itself for the first time in decades.

It was plainly ridiculous for the Government to expect the railways to operate at full capacity while permitting their male staff to leave in such numbers. Even when the Army appears to have grudgingly acknowledged that the railways should be able to recall former staff unsuitable for foreign service, it proved almost impossible for the companies to bring back those whom the Army might have designated as unfit for service overseas. Edwin Pratt recorded that, although this was a reasonable request, 'the companies got back very few, if, indeed, any at all, of the men in question'.

* * *

Recent studies of women's work on the railways have categorised relief work at wayside stations as 'employment', where tea and other refreshments would be provided for troop trains stopping on the way to embarkation. The sheer scale of provisions suggests a full-time operation, but there was obviously a great deal of voluntary work involved, probably drawn from better-off classes of society.

But this was not the same thing as work undertaken full-time on the railway, much of it usually of a menial nature – carriage cleaning, wagon loading and unloading, or machine operation in the company works. Ticket collecting was included, but perhaps the most senior was the post of stationmaster (stationmistress?) held by a lady on the Lancashire & Yorkshire at Irlams o' the Heights. There is evidence that many women found more well-paid, challenging tasks in railway service than they would have done otherwise, while even menial jobs working for a commercial company were preferable to domestic service. One woman working as an assistant purser on an inshore railway steamer accepted a cleaning post on the railways in 1919 rather than return to domestic drudgery subject to the dictates, even the whims, of a private employer.

The contribution made by women, on the railways and in munitions, was surely more instrumental in converting contemporary opinion to favour emancipation of women than the years of Suffragette activity had achieved. An alternative theory exists among the more cynical of psephologists that politicians hurriedly granted women the vote in the 1918 General Election because of the logistical impossibility of collecting servicemen's votes overseas, thus leaving a victorious party open to a charge of taking power on a severely limited franchise. Women's assistance in running the railways is a more attractive theory.

But Edwin Pratt summed up women's contribution to railway service with words that can be viewed as, at the very least, inappropriate, or at their worst, downright morbid. This was a negative description, written by Pratt when describing the main memorial service for fallen railwaymen at St Paul's Cathedral in 1919 (with this author's italics and punctuation): 'It was their [women's] readiness to take up railway work in a great variety of forms which had *enabled* many of those, in whose memory the service was being held, to join the forces and make the sacrifice of their lives for the Great Cause in which they fought'.

On a more prosaic level it may well be that, by accident or design, the Government managed to make a timely intervention into the manpower 'market'. Had women not been introduced into transport jobs from the second quarter of 1915, it is doubtful if so many could have been recruited a year later, when the ROFs opened their doors, and offered wages that were so much higher. That maintaining gender and age balances in the workplace was essential in this war becomes evident when historians' verdicts on its outcome are considered. Historian David Stevenson believes that in 1918 'the German army ran out of men … too few women and too many able-bodied younger males were committed to war production'.

Arsenal Cities

As its name suggest, the Arsenal has traditionally been the principal producer of munitions to feed the guns of Army and Navy since the seventeenth century. Based at a site covering 1,300 acres at Woolwich on the south bank of the Thames, it geared up in 1914 by increasing its staff to no fewer than 70,000. With stations for both the munitions plant and the dockyard of the same name, it was well connected by rail on the SE&CR's North Kent line.

Its wartime rail traffic included 3.5 million wagon workings in and out of its sidings, which were almost overwhelmed with the traffic. There were only nine sidings available at the outset of war, with nine more added by June 1915, as part of a programme by the railway company to lay an additional 12 miles of siding. At one stage of the war, up to 2,000 wagons, loaded and empty, were having to be processed at the Arsenal and its associated dockyard, and some stabling of rolling stock had to be undertaken on nearby running-lines, with normal traffic being reduced to virtual branch-line operation. Five actual branches were closed before 1916, and five more after Haig's call for yet more help from the railways after the Battle of the Somme. All this was according to Edwin Pratt, who records that the South Eastern established a control centre at London Bridge, followed by other centres at Dartford and Tonbridge. He does not mention if the company had difficulty in obtaining the necessary telephone wire, a commodity finding its way to the Front in increasing amounts, and making it difficult for other railways attempting to introduce much-needed traffic control.

By the spring of 1915 it became obvious that there was going to be a shortage in heavy ordnance if the warring powers were to continue their attack methods, which consisted of bombarding the enemy trenches with artillery for hours on end (in later battles, for days on end) and then marching one's own troops towards what were presumed to be defences deserted and destroyed. More and more shells would be required – before three attacks in 1917 in excess of 10 million rounds were fired, at a manufactured cost of more than £53 million – and all expended in support of actions which advanced the Front Line by only a few miles. The most rounds fired in a single twenty-four-hour period totalled 943,847, costed at £3.87 million, at the end of September 1918, according to the official volume *Statistics of the Military Effort of the British Empire*. Obviously, the creation of a Ministry of Munitions had been an unchallengeable necessity.

This was established in May 1915, very much as a result of agitation by the Chancellor of the Exchequer, David Lloyd George. It seems surprising that so many of his contemporaries regarded him as a political opportunist – none more so than Margot Asquith, wife of the Prime Minister – when he was in fact prepared to resign one of the highest offices of state and personally establish a new ministry with a technological base, but little in the way of political prestige. The story persists of Lloyd George arriving at an unused building allocated to him in Whitehall and stopping workmen from removing furniture. It was typical of a man who had grasped the nature of total war, and the necessity for a nation to think in exclusively martial terms.

* * *

As if to prove that the railways' thirty-two workshops represented a major part of Britain's engineering capacity, Lloyd George requested a meeting with the Railway Works Manufacturing Committee within ten days of taking his ministerial oath. On 24 June he asked the distinguished CMEs on the committee for 2,000 6-inch calibre shells to be delivered each week. Seven of the largest companies agreed to supply even more than this – 2,500 weekly, if they could have certain 'turners and machinemen' returned to them from the services. This was apparently agreed to, and the Great Western, London & North Western, L&Y, North Eastern, Great Northern, Great Central, and Great Eastern all contracted to supply the required amount of projectiles to hurl at the enemy. In addition, the first two of these companies undertook to produce castings, which would allow a wider array of manufacturers to become involved in the future.

Arrangements for the payment for all this was somewhat muddled to begin with, as weapons manufacture could hardly be regarded as a normal activity for a railway company whose profits were being maintained at peacetime levels. At one early stage of the new ministry's life it appeared that it would pay the companies directly, not just for munitions, but also for ambulance trains. This latter point was clearly inappropriate, and the War Office soon confirmed that it would pay for these, and later also for such trains supplied for the use of US forces towards the end of the war. When Edwin Pratt was interviewing railway managers for his book published in 1921, the restoring of ambulance carriages for normal passenger use was still being undertaken and remained to be costed.

Finally, the 1915 contact between railways and the new minister resulted in railway workshops supplying £500,000 worth of castings for well over 100 commercial engineering firms, most of them small, but headed by Vickers, Coventry Ordnance, and Armstrong Whitworth. By the end of the war, thirty-two railway workshops had contributed munitions and appropriate metalwork for weapons forging to the tune of £17.8 million. This was in addition to supporting the main drive of Lloyd George's vision – what might be described as 'arsenal cities', but historically known as Royal Ordnance Factories.

* * *

Here thousands worked, and in many cases lived; the size of the workforce was too big for any non-urban area to provide. Their task was to answer the needs of a nation suddenly desperate for war materials to fire at an enemy whom Britain had clearly underestimated. Making this all the more urgent was the fact that the existing Arsenal at Woolwich was well within the reach of the Zeppelin, not to mention later Gothas and Giants. By February 1915 London found itself being bombed from the air, a concept so original that many civilian casualties resulted simply because overawed citizens rushed into the unprotected streets simply to gawp at the silver monsters overhead. But the whole nation was unprotected at first, and the bombing campaign, and the meagre efforts made to combat it, are described later.

As well as placing orders with existing factories, whether commercial engineering firms or railway works, the new ministry needed its manufacturing capacity located at sites with good transport links, a water supply, and all well out of the bombers' reach. (In later years, the Air Council of Great Britain drew a line on a map, from the Bristol Channel to Linlithgow near Edinburgh, and decided that everything west of there would be safe from aerial bombing. In 1934 nobody expected airfields in France and the Low Countries to be used by an enemy air force, as happened only six years later.) Sixteen factories were under construction by the end of July 1915, with no fewer than 250 established by the end of the war.

One such ROF site was at Gretna, straddling the Anglo-Scottish border to an extent of some 7 linear miles. John Reith, recovering from a wound received on the Western Front, was involved in the planning required for this enormous site, although he was not present when surveyors began their work, only to have a prize bull turned on them by a local farmer who had not been notified of the contribution his district was about to make to the war effort. One of the biggest ROFs in the Second World War was at Chorley in Lancashire, with 35,000 workers. Gretna would employ only 5,000 fewer than that some twenty-five years earlier.

Gretna's construction from the autumn of 1915 produced a transformation in a district lacking even an electricity supply – which might have excused the Caledonian for not fitting track circuiting at Quintinshill, the site of Britain's worst railway accident only a mile or so to the north, and surely preventable if track circuiting had been in use. The Caledonian company had a station at Gretna, on the WCML some 9 miles from Carlisle, and just before the junction with the Glasgow & South Western, which also had a Gretna station. The North British had a tiny terminus here too, all to serve a local population of barely 2,000. Historian Edwin Pratt is not entirely clear which of the three passenger stations he was referring to when he reported that 8,653 tickets were sold at Gretna in the whole of 1914 – a figure down on the previous year's. Three years later, the numbers using the station or stations came to 2.9 *million*.

This was despite the fact that two-thirds of the workforce was accommodated on site, using the internal rail system – of which there were two, of standard and narrow gauge – to travel to and from whichever factory building where they worked. There were 40 route miles of standard gauge internally, with an additional 36 miles of sidings, as well as 49 miles in narrower gauges. Dormitories had to be provided, along with churches, reservoir, telephone exchange, and a cinema. A power station was built, powering an electric main 20 miles in length, while the internal roads stretched for 30 miles. Local quarries were called on to provide building material, and the Caledonian was best-placed to supply the stone requiring transport. A Gretna township station was built, providing the area with its fourth. That many workers were also forced to commute daily to the ROF was shown by the necessity of the nearby station of Annan having two footbridges, a second provided to handle the volume of workers alighting on the down platform at the end of the working day. John Reith commuted to and from one station farther down the line, at the now-closed Cummertrees. REC Circular 647 laid out conditions for weekend travel for munition workers wishing to visit their families, but, surprisingly perhaps, specified only men.

Specialising in cordite production from the summer of 1916, this site had a greater output than all the other manufacturing ROFs combined. Its establishment was not free of problems by any means; the REC 'Flying Squad' of Superintendents discovered no fewer than 560 wagons awaiting unloading here – probably with building materials, so early in the ROF's history. These were being unloaded at a rate of seventy per day, but a further 800 were waiting at Carlisle. There was a 'personnel' problem at Gretna too. So well paid was the workforce that pubs in the area from Carlisle to Annan had to be nationalised, to introduce regulation of alcohol consumption, and ensure that leisure facilities were provided as alternatives to the demon drink (and this control continued until the 1970s). On a national scale, new industrial centres, where workers' welfare was actually a matter of concern for management, was what the railways were having to compete with in the labour market.

It was not only factory sites that were required by Lloyd George's new ministry. In late June 1915 Britain's railways were asked if they could provide office accommodation – free of charge naturally – in eight cities: Birmingham, Bristol, Cardiff, Edinburgh, Glasgow, Leeds, Manchester, and Newcastle. Why the REC, which distributed this request for offices each capable of accommodating up to twenty staff, believed that railways would have excess space available at a time when they were working at full stretch, is unclear.

Within a year of being founded, Britain's new Ministry of Munitions would produce the equivalent of a previous year's output of ammunition in only eleven days. The number of artillery pieces increased from 3,481 in 1915 to 20,971 in 1918. Heavy guns multiplied from sixteen to 370 in that period, while the number of 'very heavy' went from 0 to 234. The Ministry may have imposed enormous demands on the nation's railways, but at least it justified its existence.

Resisting Air Attack

In September 1914, the commissioner of the Metropolitan Police called a meeting with civic and military leaders to discuss defence measures for London 'should they come'. 'They' were German aircraft, harbingers of invasion which would surely be attempted if the enemy defeated France. The new REC was represented at the meeting by Guy (later Sir Guy) Calthrop of the L&NWR, but no specific preparations were agreed upon, and the railways were clearly expected to get on with things. It is not difficult to imagine that those attending believed that the issue was probably academic.

But they proved to be wrong. Edwin Pratt's history of Britain's railways in the First World War has a chapter on attacks from the air. It is the longest in the book.

From Christmas Day 1914, with the bombing of the Midland's Tilbury–Pitsea line, it became apparent that the German forces, unable to cross the North Sea, would compensate by attacking Britain from the air. By the following February, London itself was under attack. This was a form of enemy intrusion without precedent in history. It is to the credit of the British Government at the time that there was never any question of targeting German towns and civilians, and even the Cuxhaven Raid was intended only as an attack on a naval base and its ships.

Compared to the Blitz of the Second World War, the attacks on London and other British targets were almost derisory in terms of the technology involved and the damage caused, but anti-aircraft precautions and civil defence measures were fairly risible too. A Zeppelin's crew would view their targets from a surprisingly low altitude, dropping their bombs by hand, and often failing to hit even large buildings. No railway suffered serious damage from aerial attack in the first half of the war, but civilians proved vulnerable because of their fascination with the silver monsters above, often transfixed with amazement as a bomb hurtled down towards them.

There was no fighter cover initially, no expertise in anti-aircraft gunnery, and no means of warning civilians to take cover except by lowering gas pressure in municipal lighting supply. Even that could do little to inform the public of what was coming, and what the authorities expected of them. By the end of the war, a DORA specified that a black-out must be introduced, but it was never fully effective in a society where it was difficult to disseminate information easily, and where railway yards and stations were exempted anyway – although this was apparently not observed consistently. At least in London, the public could seek refuge in the Underground.

There was confusion in how the railways should react to air raids – not surprisingly, considering the unprecedented nature of the threat. As a result, the authorities' reactions were inconsistent, and very soon, conflicting. After being told in September 1914 just to muddle along, one railway, the South Eastern, was suddenly informed that it must dowse lights and stop running all trains when raiders were approaching. Chaos resulted, out of all proportion to the damage suffered. Perhaps not surprisingly, a policy of 'business as usual' began to creep back into rail operations. But some criticism of this at a conference in September 1915, chaired by American-born H. W. Thornton, GM of the Great Eastern Railway, came from a single high-ranking Royal Flying Corps (RFC) officer, and the policy changed again. Once more a decision was made to stop all traffic, this time nationally, when raiders had been detected. This was of course exactly the procedure followed in the Second World War, although that involved more low-level attacking.

But in January 1916, the station staff at London's Victoria realised that suspending rail movements, possibly because of air raids far from the capital, had resulted in some 4,000 passengers having to 'shelter' under the glass roof of the terminus during one alarm. And all because of a small fire started following a bombing raid at Dudley in Warwickshire. While this caused little damage (and was the Great Western's only incident), there were repercussions for the latter company, whose passenger services were delayed by a total of 195 hours and goods trains by 650 hours. A conference was organised shortly afterwards, attended by the REC, War Office, RFC, and GHQ Home Forces, concluding that slow running of trains would be preferable to a standstill. So, policy changed again, and unlike conditions on the railways in the next conflict, rail traffic was not brought to a complete stop during raids, although passenger trains could not exceed 15 mph or goods trains, 10 mph.

With the question settled of how to (indeed, whether to) operate trains during raids, there were three REC directives in the early summer of 1916 on how to compensate railway staff in the event of injury or death during air raids. The companies were not liable under the existing legislation, the Workers' Compensation Act, but, according to REC Circular 580 'seeing that the War Office have requested that traffic on the Railways should be suspended as little as possible during the Raids ... it will be rather hard to refuse to compensate men who are injured in the course of their duties (or their representatives if they are killed)'.

But it was to be stressed to staff that any payment made in these circumstances would be voluntary on the part of the employer, and no liability was implied. A later circular asked companies to inform the REC of any compensation payments already made.

* * *

At one of the conferences in 1915, the railways had reasonably requested that the military should improve its system for warning them of forthcoming raids. As a result, from April 1916, there was a concerted civil defence initiative, with the Headquarters Home Forces passing advance warnings about developing raids to local authorities and the REC. The latter then informed the companies in the regions threatened – England and Wales was divided into forty-three administrative areas and Scotland ten – and coordinated the collection of information afterwards. Curiously, in Scotland the North British Railway was tasked with acting as information coordinator, in place of the REC. Not that official warnings consisted of much more than 'Brace yourself – here they come'.

Despite this impotence, or perhaps because of the authorities' consciousness of it, the warning procedure for air raids became progressively more bureaucratic by the summer of 1916. The REC listed fourteen companies who would be contacted directly in the event of an attack in any of the forty-three areas, these railways being the eleven English companies on the management committee plus two of the London underground networks and the Midland's Tilbury section (the recently taken-over London Tilbury & Southend). These were known as 'Category One' companies, with the second of these categories comprising smaller railways who would notified by the nearest large network, for example, the Cambrian would receive information from the Great Western, should the raiders have reached that far west. Category Three were twenty-three small companies who would receive a call from the military over 'Post Office Telephone lines'. Since they included the Midland & Great Northern Joint, with much of its mileage on the North Sea coast, it would appear that the arrangements were still imperfect, if not downright confused.

Also occupying the east coast, the Great Eastern undertook detailed record-keeping of the routes used by enemy aircraft, apparently to assist the military to identify the enemy's likely bombing paths and preferred meteorological conditions in future. The GER's collection of data included barometer observations, and this soon proved useful – if only to confirm what must have seemed obvious – that raiders were more likely to arrive 'on a rising barometer of about 30 inches'. This was supposedly to coincide with a 'retrograde' measurement on the return journey, in other words worsening conditions likely to discourage pursuing fighters. How the Germans could be assured of this meteorological progression was not clear.

Anticipating attacks in moonlight conditions was fairly predictable, and after a raid in April 1916, even the planet Venus was blamed for providing as much illumination as the Moon would have done! But it was impossible for the company to confidently identify Zeppelin 'highways' across the eastern counties. Contemporary historians do not mention – and may have been unaware of the fact – that aircrew would frequently use railway lines to navigate by. Even at night or in poor light conditions, glare from a firebox, or plumes of steam, could draw attention to the existence of a line, and rails reflecting moonlight were also a guide to the airman. In later air operations in the years between the wars, it was not uncommon for civil pilots to 'navigate' by rail.

Between Christmas 1914 and mid-June 1918 there were 108 air attacks on Britain, split almost exactly half-and-half between airship and aeroplane, and peaking in 1916. The farthest west reached by Zeppelin was on the 'wrong' side of Shrewsbury, an achievement which appears to have been overlooked by future defence planners in 1934 (as mentioned in the account of Arsenal Cities). By the end of the war, the Germans had replaced the slow-moving Zeppelin with Gotha and Giant aircraft, the latter with four engines and improved bomb delivery systems. Fortunately, their introduction was followed by the failure of Ludendorff's offensive on the Western Front, despite using troops released from the east following the withdrawal of Russia from the war. The tide was turning at last, with the Allied armies now supplemented by the entry of American troops. One of the last Zeppelin raids was in March 1918, and it was the Hartlepools which experienced it.

* * *

Perhaps the most important main line which could be damaged, or even put out of action, from the air was the East Coast Main Line (ECML). Almost all of its entire 520-mile length was within airship range of Germany, and there were a number of viaducts whose destruction could have caused major logistical problems, as well as battering British prestige. Welwyn, Durham, the two Tyne viaducts, the Royal Border, and the Forth Bridge were all likely targets, although curiously where these were guarded by sentries it was to protect them from possible Sinn Fein attack. The Forth Bridge represented the most northerly target, proving too well defended by naval guns for two Zeppelins attacking in April 1916. Indeed, the whole route did not have to record a single death among passengers or railwaymen from air raids. (An off-duty lady typist employed by the NER was, however, unfortunately killed in York.)

The most southerly of three companies making up the route, the Great Northern, was hampered by its cheerful readoption of excursion tickets in September 1914, when it would have been more logical to abandon the scheme for the duration, instead of having to honour any cheap tickets already bought, right up until December. And unlike its two partner companies on the ECML, the GNR did suffer some damage from air raids, but no staff were killed or wounded by enemy action while on duty.

King's Cross station received attention from the enemy, although the most damage, to a passenger guard's van in the terminus in September 1917, was caused by 'friendly fire' – a falling shell, presumably fired by an anti-aircraft gun. Passenger trains already filled were taken into the tunnels immediately after a warning was received, and the only damage experienced was to paving outside the station, and to signal wires in North London. Clerical staff at King's Cross were expected to remain at their posts during raids – not an unreasonable demand when the terminus roof had reportedly been reinforced, and most bombs were so light as to be dropped by hand.

When war ended in November 1918, the GNR could look back on a proud record of service, with 60 per cent of their passengers travelling in uniform, and with trains filled to capacities previously undreamed of. The maximum crowded into a single train was 1,625 – bigger than the average regimental battalion. Three million wagon loads were exchanged, during the Great War, between the Great Northern and its northern neighbour, the North Eastern, most of them at Shaftholme Junction.

The North Eastern Railway itself, as the link between north and south on the ECML, received forty air-raid warnings in the First World War, although seventeen of these were false alarms. Most bombs fell in the Humber area, although three were dropped on York, while such coastal communities as

Scarborough, Whitby, Hartlepool, and Seaham experienced bombardments from German warships offshore. None of the aerial attacks directly affected the company's infrastructure or rolling stock, and no NER railwayman was killed by bombing. Unfortunately, three employees died from shellfire in December 1914.

Traffic doubled on the company's network during war, with 24,172 extra passenger specials being operated – approximately twenty per day in every six-day week. The NER was the secretary company to the Army's Northern Command, and of course serviced one of the largest infantry camps in the UK, at Catterick, on the Richmond branch, with Darlington as its ECML change station. Service personnel totalling 11.8 million were moved in the fifty-one months of war, but the number of auxiliary and industrial support workers carried came to no less than 83.5 million.

Wagon loads exchanged with the NBR on the ECML doubled in the Up direction and increased even more, by 182 per cent, in the northbound (although there was also a secondary route wending its way through Hexham, the Border Counties line, and the Waverley Route). These figures do not include the movement of 'Admiralty' coal, which had to be transported from South Wales to Scottish North Sea ports for onward movement to Scapa Flow. This traffic was shared with the WCML, and to a lesser extent, even the Midland's Settle–Carlisle line, along with the consequent movement of returning empties.

Continuing northwards, we find that at the NBR operational headquarters of Edinburgh Waverley, the station's importance had been increased by the installation of a continuously open telephone line from Scottish Command at nearby Edinburgh Castle. This was part of a communications system to warn relevant railways of incoming air raids from Zeppelins (and the castle itself experienced bombing, one of the 'near misses' unfortunately resulting in nine civilian deaths nearby). The committee's staff undertook this in England and Wales, but the NBR was specified as responsible for warning all Scotland's railways whenever it was informed by Coastal Command HQ (not to be confused with the later RAF Coastal Command) that German airships were on their way. Happily the existing military telephone link did not become overloaded, with Scotland only undergoing one major raid. No railway staff north of the Border were killed, or NBR services interrupted, although David L. Smith, unofficial historian of the Glasgow & South Western, recorded that all that company's services were brought to a halt on one occasion when an excitable signalman swore that Zeppelins were attacking on the Solway Coast, well to the west.

* * *

While the Great Northern's London terminus survived unscathed, it was a different matter 'next door' when St Pancras, the Midland's Grand Hotel and Somers Town goods depot were bombed by five aircraft in February 1918. Eight out of the ten fatalities caused by bombing here were railwaymen, with twenty-seven wounded. Passenger services were, however, unaffected. Another terminus had an even worse experience when the Great Eastern's Liverpool Street station was bombed by a force of no fewer than fourteen bombers. A loaded passenger train for Hunstanton was damaged, as was a coach used as a recruiting centre for railwaymen. Ten railway staff died out of a total of sixteen, and thirty-six were injured altogether, in the worst bombing attack on the railways in the First World War. The existence of a mobile recruiting centre for railwaymen, actually for medical checks, suggests that REC Circular 61, from the second month of war, was forgotten while the Army sought manpower everywhere as it prepared for yet another 'big push'.

London's Underground network was heavily used as a sanctuary by an understandably frightened population. Some 4.25 million Londoners took refuge in the Tube system during the war, including 300,000 on one particular date, 18 February 1918. On one occasion in the previous year 120,000 people sought refuge when an attack was rumoured but did not in fact take place. The companies accepted this influx on thirty occasions, but posters in the stations warned those taking shelter that they occupied the stations at their own risk, and special constables were recruited to maintain order. The systems, then still privately owned, appear to have kept running throughout, and some enterprising Londoners bought tickets on the Circle Line and sat in comparative warmth and comfort until it was deemed safe to return to their homes.

Hotels

No fewer than twenty rail companies owned hotels, with no relation between the size of the company and the number of establishments it operated. Indeed, the smaller companies often prided themselves on their hotel ownership. The Glasgow & South Western owned six, equalled by the Great Northern and beaten only by the Midland, with eleven, and the North Western, with eight. It obviously paid those companies operating in the more scenic parts of the UK to offer hotel services – so the Highland owned five, plus a shared ownership, while the Furness and the Dublin & South Eastern both operated in the hospitality industry. With the public being discouraged from travelling from August 1914 – although the message was not loud and clear, particularly towards day trippers – the companies were only too glad to see their hotels being taken over for other uses.

The Great Eastern's four establishments illustrate the variety of uses made of railway hotels. At London's Liverpool Street, the Great Eastern continued a 'business as usual' policy. It was not taken over by the military, but obviously found a considerable passing trade catering for the needs of both Army and Navy officers travelling to and from East Anglia. At Harwich the company's hotel became an Army hospital, serving in that function until 1919. The nearby

Parkeston Quay Hotel accommodated RN officers, while the Sandringham at Hunstanton became a brigade headquarters for the Army.

Elsewhere in London, the Hotel Great Central at Marylebone, with its cycle track on the top floor, was taken over by the Army, and here Siegfried Sassoon underwent a medical assessment to decide whether he was fit to return to the Front in May 1917. He later described the examining doctor as 'sadistic' at the HGC for trying to tempt patients to request more time to recover, and immediately claiming this as a sign of fitness, of logic, and a heightened awareness of danger. This was the kind of 'Catch 22' test more usually followed at medical tribunals in hospitals, not in railway hotels.

At the other end of the kingdom, the Highland ran five and one-third hotels, at Inverness, Dornoch, Kyle, Achnasheen, Strathpeffer, and with a shared ownership in the Station Hotel at Perth. Again, there was variety in the wartime use of these establishments – Strathpeffer accommodated a Young Officers Training Centre before this was ousted in favour of a United States Naval Hospital later in the war. At Dornoch, golfers were replaced by the Gordon Highlanders, who in turn gave way to the Canadian Forestry Corps. At Kyle of Lochalsh, the Station Hotel was more predictably taken over by the Admiralty.

* * *

'Refreshment rooms', as station buffets were called, were the subject of one of the earliest REC circulars to the companies, and the fact that this was issued before the end of the first month of war in 1914 indicates their importance. It appeared that there was an anomaly in the way that meals, or even just cups of tea, were supplied to forces on the move. Naval ratings benefitted from an initiative by the Railway Clearing House in the previous March whereby a sailor would receive a meal at a station restaurant 'on surrender of a voucher, the Admiralty reimbursing the railway companies one shilling for each meal supplied'. Clearly, the authorities had not anticipated the movement of the BEF, or any other major Army moves, in the near future, and the lack of provision for soldiers had to be addressed.

REC Secretary Gilbert Szlumper, who doubled in that role for the L&SWR in normal times, asked the railway companies on 31 August to put similar arrangements in place for Army personnel, or simply provide a meal for a shilling to anyone in uniform. It was not clear if the War Office would offer to recompense the companies, or indeed if they were involved at this stage, but later troop movements had a more ordered nature, with regulations being laid down about the time of station stops (not more than thirty minutes for any one train), and taps for soldiers to fill their water bottles. The refreshment of soldiers and sailors became a growth point in rail transport, with Edwin Pratt devoting a surprising amount of space to this in his history of Britain's railways in the First World War. The scale of the catering required can be assessed from the statistic that the two

'Free Buffets' provided by the Great Eastern at London's Liverpool Street terminus provided refreshments for more than 500,000 soldiers in 1918 alone.

Women volunteers were quick to become involved, even if only, in some cases, supplying nothing more than a cup of tea, drunk by the serviceman leaning out of the carriage window. With rather more than 200 troops or sailors per train, numbers in which the BEF appears to have been transported originally, station platforms would be busy places. For example, a young soldier called George Baird, off to the Dardanelles, found his departure platform so mobbed that he could only 'glimpse' his mother at the back of the crowd. Wounded in that futile fight, he was then sent to the Western Front, where he was crippled for life. Crowded station platforms were a turmoil of stories like this.

New Traffic Streams II

When Kentish businessman William Willett published his pamphlet on daylight saving in Edwardian days, he found that, although politicians and the public found the idea fascinating, it was thought impossible to persuade an entire population to change their clocks twice yearly. His idea was that putting clocks one hour ahead in summer would allow more work to be done in daylight, thus saving fuel for lighting, as well as providing workers with a better chance of enjoying some sunlight in the early evenings. Willett's pamphlet ran to seven editions, but it was only in the dark days of total war that the protagonist nations realised the merits of such a scheme. Germany and Austria are believed to have undertaken this first, but in May 1916 Westminster passed the Summer Time Act, and on the 16th of that month the REC contacted all railway companies with instructions.

Circular 573 intimated that the first clock-change would take place at 0200 hours GMT on the morning of 21 May. This was of course much later than daylight saving is undertaken nowadays (and the twenty-four-hour clock is used here for clarity although the REC notice specified the traditional a.m./p.m. system, one used on Britain's railways until the 1960s). As might be expected, the circular explained that staff on duty at that time were responsible for putting the companies' clocks forward in the station building or signal box, unless a contractor undertook their maintenance. In the case of an unstaffed building, the last worker to go off duty was responsible for putting the clock hand once round the dial. There was no instruction for engine drivers, but guards had to log that the hour had been advanced on their watches. Any worker who lost an hour's pay because of a shift ending early should be compensated. All connections with 'mail' trains, presumably overnight services, were to be held for the extra hour, although this instruction was surely unnecessary.

Willett had believed that a one-hour change would be difficult to implement and there should be four weekly adjustments of twenty minutes each. In practice, the first change – and of course for an advance of sixty minutes – seems to have been accomplished seamlessly in a society where the average citizen was already feeling the weight of governmental authority, although changing the clocks back in the following October was more difficult for mechanistic reasons. 'Clockwork' clocks were required to have their hands moved forward by eleven hours in order to be put back by one, although the later REC instruction did not deal with this practical matter. At least railways did not require striking clocks; some householders were to find turning clocks back one hour – by going forward – to be time-consuming (no pun intended), with the clock chiming every hour during the change. But the importance of all this was made clear; railways were assured that clock-changing would 'reduce the number of hours during which artificial lighting is used in the evenings, and so save the nation fuel and oil for lighting, and release large quantities of coal which are urgently needed for other purposes arising from the War'. This was the message from the Home Secretary, displaying economic prudence in a nation whose military commanders were soon to waste a quarter of a million lives in the valley of the Somme.

* * *

As we have seen, the U-boat and the minefield caused a major rethink on how Britain would move its goods. If coastal vessels could not be expected to run the gauntlet of the North Sea to service the Grand Fleet in its Orkney Island lair, the same problems applied on the south and west coasts, once considered immune to enemy intervention. As a result, a far-reaching policy decision was made to encourage the movement of goods internally, when port-to-port by sea would have been routinely undertaken in peacetime. This took the form of an invisible subsidy in pegging railway rates at pre-war levels, while 'coastwise' shipping took on a more realistic pricing character, and by the end of hostilities was running at nearly twice railway rates. Transporting a ton of hemp from Liverpool to London early in 1919 would cost 35s by coastal steamer, but only 19s 11d by train. At this time, even after the armistice, the railways were struggling to reacquire as many as possible of the 31,000 wagons they had loaned the Army for overseas transport, and there was a shortfall of some 14,000 in the numbers of private-owner wagons available. But even long before that, the authorities had realised that this was not turning out well. Traffic had been added to the railways, its subsidised nature generating increased administration in compensating the companies involved.

In October 1915 the REC let it be known that it had 'regrettably' discovered that 400 wagonloads of hay had recently been transported from Grangemouth to Cardiff, 100 of cotton from Sharpness to Liverpool, and another 400 loads of barbed wire from Plymouth to the Royal V&A docks in London – all by rail. The second of these three examples involved locations connected by canal, but the (in many cases) pre-Victorian waterway network proved incapable of handling more modern cargoes, as discussed earlier in this volume. In any event, the point of origin of the above cargoes was surely relevant. If barbed wire was imported at Plymouth, why not into London, or a port connected with it by waterway? Suffice to say that the authorities, having interfered in the commercial conduct of internal transport, appear to have overburdened the railways, while at the same time, trying to increase traffic on the canals. One policy was too successful, the second a complete failure.

The problem of railway popularity through cheapness persisted even after the armistice. In August 1919 *The Times* carried a report that a recent London–Manchester voyage had been abandoned as only 200 tons of cargo could be assembled to transport in a vessel of 1,200 tons' capacity, the railways naturally taking up the load. But the newspaper's thunder had been stolen – two days earlier the Board of Trade had issued an order banning rail transport of import or export goods between ports, with traders able to claim a subsidy in using other means of transport, presumably involving coastal shipping. Despite this, Edwin Pratt believed that the railways' comparatively short journey times, and immunity to the vagaries of tide and weather, made their service worth paying more for, and this effort by Government to keep goods off the 'overburdened railways' was not one of its more popular measures.

* * *

Of the many accounts of special traffic arrangements in the First World War, the Great Northern's history can supply one that is particularly poignant. In June 1916, the company laid on a special train to carry Lord Kitchener and Foreign Office staff northwards on the ECML on the first stage of an important diplomatic mission to Tsarist Russia. They were due to board the cruiser HMS *Hampshire* at Scapa Flow, but their train had not long left King's Cross when it was discovered that a senior official had been left behind. At very short notice, the GNR arranged a second special in pursuit of the first. This rattled off the 155 miles to Doncaster in 149 minutes, including four minutes for engine-changing at Grantham, and another four in signalling delays, before passing its important passenger on to the NER at Shaftholme. Meanwhile, Kitchener ordered his train to wait at York – and the official 'rejoined the party, with whom he subsequently perished', as the official history reports matter-of-factly of the cruiser's fate in the waters off the Orkney Islands.

One of the REC's unstated functions was to introduce a measure of control into the military's commissioning of special train workings, where a senior officer could browbeat patriotic railway managers into laying on a special train for a single military personage. Here the GNR had made an exception in what their management thought was a matter of national importance, but Fate ruled that all this would be in vain.

* * *

New weaponry required new modes of transport. The first military tanks were operational in 1916, but, travelling at walking speed, were hardly going to reach a Channel port from their makers under their own power. Their weight made them difficult to transport, and their numbers might come as a surprise – some 2,818 were produced by the end of the war, and the L&NWR alone claimed to have moved no fewer than 3,288 by mid-1919. The Great Eastern was the company principally involved in transporting them to and from a training ground in Suffolk. Meanwhile, the movement of large guns of 15-inch calibre or more, capable of firing a shell more than 20 miles, required an improvised form of bogie wagon, with the Great Central devising a suitable transporter. Naval requirements for this kind of ordnance declined in number as the war went on, while the Army's need for big guns increased.

* * *

An unexpected complication had to be addressed in November 1916, the month when the Battle of the Somme ended, with a huge addition to the total of the nation's dead. REC Circular 748 was concerned with the transfer of officers' bodies from hospitals in the UK to their families. With battlefield dead being buried in the new mass graveyards, the REC circular dealt with those wounded and brought back to 'Blighty' for treatment. Surprisingly, it appeared that there were frequent instances of an officer's remains being transported with papers describing him as a 'soldier', which the circular pointed out meant 'Other Ranks'. Officers were not afforded free transport if dead, it appears. This was a serious problem for the families of former NCOs who had been commissioned, and, as 'temporary gentlemen', came from humbler backgrounds than that of the traditional British officer.

Sadly, inland transport by one of the many ambulance trains so promptly and proudly supplied by the railway companies was often in vain for those whose wounds were soiled by battlefield dirt. One Army surgeon was devastated by his inability to treat such contamination, and longed for an antiseptic which could tackle infection without damaging living tissue. His name was Alexander Fleming and it would need another world war before his response would be known.

British Railways at Sea

Decades have passed since the days when ships sailed British coastal waters bearing the insignia of a railway concern, whether private or nationalised. But in 1914, fourteen railway companies in Great Britain were operating steamer services, ranging from cross-Channel links with Europe and Ireland, the isles of Wight and Man, to pleasure vessels on Windermere and Loch Lomond. The 218 railway ships totalled some 69,000 tons, most of the craft being of less than 250 tons displacement, but included some of the finest Channel and Irish Sea steamers.

Railway companies carrying on business in deep waters, as well as shallow, probably seemed natural to railway managers, and not least passengers, as until around 1850 a long-distance journey was impossible (or involved a lengthy diversion) without a ferry having to be used to traverse major rivers. With so many companies commanding, in theory at least, formidable amounts of capital, it must have seemed logical for a railway to invest in shipping arrangements to ensure its passengers travelling to a port on the English Channel or Irish Sea would be guaranteed a smooth passage onwards. What *is* surprising is that the concept of train ferries – of loading the carriages or wagons of a train over a railed ramp on to the ship itself – was not universally adopted. While there were a very few examples of this in Britain in Victorian times, though it was undertaken overseas, it was an idea which had to be revived in the midst of the First World War, and was to remain in daily operation for another half century.

But this is only one facet of railway shipping. The whole subject deserves more attention, and the author makes no apology for recounting this aspect of transport history at some length, for it is a remarkable record of dedication and achievement, which the book *For the King's Service* was designed to record. In 1914 the usual perils of the sea were about to be supplemented by contact mines, torpedoes, and marauding destroyers.

Firstly, a summary of the companies and the services they offered, starting in the south-east corner of Great Britain, nearest to the gunfire:

South Eastern & Chatham Railway: Cross-Channel ferries from Kent.
London Brighton & South Coast: Cross-Channel ferries from Newhaven, described as 'The Royal Mail Route'.

London & South Western: Cross-Channel and Channel Islands operations.

Great Western: Operating from Weymouth, Plymouth and Fishguard to the Channel Islands, France, and Ireland.

London & North Western: Irish Sea operations, sometimes advertised in conjunction with the L&Y. Share of Stranraer–Larne operations.

Lancashire & Yorkshire: Active on both Irish Sea and North Sea operations.

Midland: Services from Heysham to Ireland and the Isle of Man, also controlling ownership of the Stranraer–Larne ferry station after 1907.

Furness: Irish Sea operations and Lake District pleasure sailings.

Glasgow & South Western: Firth of Clyde operations. Share of Stranraer–Larne operations.

Caledonian: Firth of Clyde, and share of Stranraer–Larne operations.

North British: Operations on Clyde, Forth, and, for a time, Irish Sea.

North Eastern: Mercantile operations through commercial flag carriers, but also tug ownership.

Great Central: North Sea operations, mainly to Baltic ports.

Great Eastern: North Sea operations to Belgian and Dutch ports.

Additionally, the Cambrian possessed legal powers to operate steamer services to and from Ireland, but these were not in use in 1914.

* * *

With all main-line railways immediately taken over by the Railway Executive Committee in 1914, their ship fleets were now effectively Government controlled, as opposed to the Admiralty's approach to the companies on a ship-by-ship basis. Assurances against financial and shipwreck loss required to be discussed, a dialogue that was to be ongoing. On the first of these points, the railways were offered guaranteed ship earnings equal to their net revenue of 1913, while, on the second, the Government would be responsible for all ship losses due to 'war risks'. This was to prove a definition open to question, since all voyages, even in peacetime, were potentially dangerous in the days before radio and radar, satellite navigation and weather forecasting. The railways would be responsible for the 'ordinary' risks posed by the sea, unless a ship had been diverted from its usual routes for military reasons – which was frequently to be the case. There is evidence of ships being 'commandeered' at short notice, but not being considered 'requisitioned'. The L&NWR's *Anglia* was lost in tragic circumstances when ferrying war wounded, but was not nominally requisitioned at that particular time.

Compensation for loss at sea was a subject not easily settled, and REC circulars were still featuring the subject long after war had been declared. In November 1916, the railways were told in Circular 729 that 'direct cash payments will not be made by the Admiralty, War Office, or Ministry of Munitions, the cost being charged in normal course to working expenses and recovered through the operation of guarantee'. In other words, the REC would undertake to pass on compensation, although this would still leave the military to deal with non-railway shipowners, hardly a satisfactory procedure for any of those concerned. Not surprisingly, the Ministry of Shipping was established before the year was out (and re-established in 1939 within two months of the Second World War being declared). Incidentally, no one could accuse the REC of sentimentality in their consideration of marine loss. The citing of compensation arrangements for the loss of railway ships was listed by the committee in a table below the loss of income from rental premises, or through the compulsory carriage of timber.

Not all shipping lines insured with Lloyd's, indeed Great Central historian George Dow believed that this company was one of the 'very few' railways to do so. Interestingly, when the Great Central lost its steamer *Immingham* in support of the Dardanelles campaign, it requested £100,000 compensation. It had to settle for £45,000. Some inconsistency emerged over the years: the loss of the G&SWR's paddle steamer *Mars*, a vessel ten years older than the *Immingham* and one-third of its value on a ton-for-ton comparison, was compensated with payment of £38,600.

As the war went on, allowance was also made for companies having to seek replacement vessels to maintain the more important ferry or trading routes when they had lost most of their fleet to the military. The alternative to this might have been for the Admiralty to take only a particular number, or proportion, of ships from each company, and here the Railway Executive Committee could have been expected to play a more active role. It hardly seemed worthwhile having a dedicated committee structure, such as the REC, liaising between railways and the military, if it could not solve such elementary problems as over-reliance on one particular company's fleet while another's had capacity available.

But any 'evening-up' was left to the companies themselves; an obvious example was the Great Eastern's chartering of Great Central vessels from early in the conflict, the former company facing increased traffic challenges to the Netherlands, while the latter had lost its German destinations. The Great Central itself was forced to charter at one stage of the war. Unable to repair a dredger because all Humber yards were already working to capacity, the GCR hired a Tilbury-based vessel (from a non-railway source). Unfortunately, it was mined on its voyage northwards to the Humber, and the North Eastern's dredger *Lord Joicey* was hurriedly chartered to replace it. As previously mentioned, the Great Western had four ferries taken off a single route, Weymouth–Channel Islands, in the first October of the war – and one was lost within four months. Not surprisingly, historian James Hamilton described the Admiralty, which had requisitioned sixty-four railway ships by the end of October 1914, as 'a continuing menace'!

It certainly appears that in most cases the Admiralty dealt directly with the companies themselves, without any reference to the REC even when it was fully established, and, as Pratt pointed out, 'without any regard for the ability of the said companies to provide for essential services they were under obligation to maintain'. Making this bullishness all the more remarkable was the fact that the 1871 Act did not mention ships at all among the railway companies' 'plant' which the military could call upon, but the vessels' inclusion among those suitable for taking up from trade seems to have been non-negotiable.

The Admiralty even advised that some vessels might not be returned at all, those which the naval authorities decided to retain being treated as losses for compensation purposes. Restoration was also a Government responsibility, with the companies to be given a twice-yearly report on the state of their ships while in military use, although there was a warning that it might not be worthwhile to repair or restore certain vessels after the Royal Navy had finished with them, never mind the enemy! Nevertheless, the six-monthly frequency timetable for reports gives an interesting contrast to the then-popular conception that the war would be over by Christmas 1914.

As the war ground on year after year, the Admiralty recognised the need to deal with the REC as a unitary body representing, among others, the fourteen ship-owning companies, and even offered to underwrite any excessive inter-company hiring costs. This was a belated recognition that the requisition of ships should have been regulated in the first place, in a manner which would have allowed the continuation of vital ferry stations, such as Harwich–Hook of Holland – which was seriously affected by GER ship unavailability – and those connecting the Kent ports with the Continent. As it was, the Admiralty was now offering a subvention to any railway company paying 'over the odds' to hire another company's ships – a curious commitment when there had been no instance of any railway concern trying to take advantage of another's loss.

The lack of an overall transport ministry must have become an increasingly obvious problem as the war went on, and its establishment does appear to have been something of a priority for Lloyd George's government, elected in December 1918. The ministry became a legal reality on 15 August 1919, its title during the parliamentary stages being the 'Ministry of Ways and Communications'. Sir Eric Geddes, previously assistant GM of the North Eastern Railway, who later rose to a Cabinet post as First Lord of the Admiralty, was the first head of this department.

* * *

Judging by four accidents on the railways in 1916–18, little thought was given to safety measures when transporting munitions by train, but by the end of the war, a regulation had been introduced regarding the carriage of explosives on railway steamers. A passenger vessel could only carry explosive material up to a certain weight limit, and only 'in a readily accessible place on deck for immediate discharge overboard' in the event of emergency. This was doubly dangerous – to handle explosives in any kind of emergency conditions such as a fire, or on a pitching deck in a storm, could result in unimaginable damage, injury, or death. Passenger vessels should not be carrying such material anyway, as, apart from obvious safety concerns, it would convert the ship into a legitimate military target if she was boarded by the enemy and the practice was discovered. Nowadays we live in an age dominated by an often derided 'health and safety' culture, but the opposite state of affairs, of the somewhat casual attitude to transporting explosives in the First World War by sea and land, was indefensible.

***

Almost all the rail companies operating ships, either directly or through an 'arm's length' company, lost vessels in the First World War. But there is no suggestion that the railways bore a disproportionate or unfair burden in the supply of ships taken up. The non-railway Isle of Man Steam Packet Company for example gave up eleven of its fifteen steamers, and one was lost. What *was* unfair was the fact that railway seamen were paid less than their fellow sailors. Not until 1918 did the Railway Executive Committee direct that seagoing railway staff must be paid at the equivalent rates recognised by the Ministry of Shipping. There was only a few weeks' backdating, but at least it was the righting of a terrible wrong. With there being virtually no danger of invasion in the UK, and only comparatively light casualties from aerial bombing, the railway companies might reasonably have recognised that the actions of U-boats or the laying of mines had made railway staff's lives so much more endangered at sea.

What follows in this extended chapter is an account of each company's contribution, rather than the chronological treatment adopted by this author in his book *For the King's Service: Railway Ships at War*. In the First World War there was little geographical progression in the maritime conflict – in other words, once the Belgian ports had been lost to Germany late in 1914, Allied ships would still operate in and out of the same ports in the North Sea, Atlantic, and Mediterranean, although with the addition of Arctic waters latterly – in contrast to the next conflict, where French ports, then much of the Mediterranean, then the Far East, were lost to Allied shipping. But for the first time, in 1914 even merchant vessels were menaced by submarines, mines, and high-speed torpedo boats. How they coped is here treated on a company-by-company basis clockwise round the British coastline, beginning with the company nearest to the slaughter of the Western Front.

***

The South Eastern & Chatham, hereafter the South Eastern, was able to claim the delivery, by rail and steamer, of the first British soldiers in France, transferred in the company's own vessel, *Hythe*. Sadly, this vessel was lost in the following year when supporting the Dardanelles campaign. By the end of the conflict, South Eastern staff was operating three train ferries out of Richborough, the specially commissioned wartime port in Kent. Originally crewed by the Inland Waterways & Docks section of the Royal Engineers in 1917, these ugly but highly useful vessels allowed rolling stock to be shunted straight on to railed decks, undoubtedly facilitating the transfer of locomotives to France in response to Haig's plea from the Somme.

The most eye-catching contribution by the South Eastern marine arm was made by three of its fast turbine-driven steamers, *Empress*, *Riviera* and *Engadine*. Their speed made them suitable for fleet work, so they were adapted to accommodate two aircraft hangars, later reduced to a stern hangar only. (To the dismay of their owners, the company archives revealed that there was doubt if they could ever again be used as ferries.) As seaplane carriers, stopping to lower and recover their aircraft to and from the sea, they could offer the fleet eyes over the horizon, although this meant introducing them into naval actions.

Two took part in the Cuxhaven Raid in 1914, a unique occasion when naval forces attacked the German coast, but the ships' aircraft failed to reach their target, the pilots contenting themselves with bombing, by hand, what German warships they could find. Unsurprisingly the attack was not a success, but the company's roll of honour was especially illuminated during the Battle of Jutland at the end of May 1916. Accompanying Admiral Beatty's scouting force, HMS *Engadine* offered a spy-in-the-sky facility (which was not utilised properly), and the South Eastern's vessel must have been in considerable danger, having to stop to operate aircraft, all the while representing the only non-armoured ship on either side in, or on the fringes of, battle. *Engadine* went on to distinguish herself at Jutland by rescuing 675 men from the sinking cruiser HMS *Warrior* and landing them safely at Rosyth. Happily, all three ships confounded their owners' fears about their modifications, resuming their peacetime role from 1919 onwards without difficulty.

Another SE&CR company ship with an impressive war record was the *Biarritz*, commissioned into the Navy straight out of the shipyard in 1915. Despite not having been designed for the deadly task of minelaying, she was credited as one of the most prolific 'sowers' in the war. One historian claims she was responsible for seriously damaging the two German capital ships that attempted to operate out of the Black Sea on behalf of Turkey. One world war was not enough for the *Biarritz*, which also took part in the second, when she was active at Dunkirk and off the Normandy beaches. All this maritime activity by the South Eastern was in addition to carrying on the more mundane task of cross-Channel services, principally in support of the military. In so doing, company losses included the historic turbine steamer *The Queen*, audaciously sunk by a German destroyer patrol barely halfway across the English Channel. At least there were no casualties, rules of chivalry being observed, and, as they awaited rescue in their lifeboats, the crew and passengers were able to contemplate the Royal Navy's failure to undertake escort duties.

To service what they advertised as the 'Royal Mail route' to Paris, the London Brighton & South Coast Railway shared ownership of a number of steamers with a French company, totalling twenty in all, including a high proportion of turbine vessels, as well as jointly owning Isle of Wight ferries with the L&SWR. After the Admiralty had called, by 1915 this total was down to four steamers of more than 250 tons' displacement, and six were jointly owned. Four of this company's ships were lost in the war, and one – the *Sussex* – co-owned with a French company, was badly damaged in 1916, but managed to reach port after being torpedoed near the French coast. Few mercantile ships could survive being struck by torpedo, but the *Sussex*, beached at Boulogne without her bow, was repaired. Newhaven appears to have been a popular attraction for U-boat commanders – in the final year of war three steamers, one of them the *Anjou*, jointly owned with the LB&SCR's French trading partner, were sunk when leaving the port, apparently without protection. The company even attained an unwanted distinction when her paddle steamer *Duchess of Richmond* became the last pre-Grouping railway-owned ship to be mined. She sank in the Aegean on 28 June 1919.

Next along the coast was the London & South Western, whose Southampton Docks complex had waved the BEF off to France and would continue to be a major transporter of officers to and from the Front in the next four years. Describing itself as 'The Military Line', with connections to 176 camps, the company enjoyed a high mercantile 'profile' owning no fewer than thirteen ships over 250 tons' displacement in 1915, with six smaller vessels owned and a further six co-owned. Six of the larger company ships took part in the movement of the BEF, and, surprisingly, the South Western recommenced civilian operations as early as 19 September in that first year. In the circumstances, the company was luckier than most in not losing a ship to enemy action until the final year of war.

Although not operated by the South Western, a train ferry facility was introduced late in the war to connect the company's quays at Southampton (Town) and (West) with any one of Le Havre, Dieppe and Cherbourg. Crewed by the Inland Waterways & Docks section of the Royal Engineers, this vessel allowed the loading of rail vehicles 'on their own wheels' on to tracks on a through deck. A similar system was developed at Richborough, and was a welcome alternative to loading and unloading of cargoes, particularly at a time when specialised labour battalions had had to be formed.

The Great Western went to sea at Weymouth, Plymouth and Fishguard, serving respectively the Channel Islands, Brest in France, and southern ports in Ireland. At Plymouth, the company also serviced ocean liners with tenders – small vessels which carried passengers and luggage to and from ships too large, or on too tight a schedule, to dock. And it was two such tender vessels that had the honour of being the first to be 'called up' when Britain went to war. Named for two historic figures associated with Plymouth, the *Sir Walter Raleigh* and *Sir Francis Drake* were in naval hands before the month of July had passed, and several days before the official declaration of war. These gallant little vessels were utilised at Scapa Flow – in both world wars.

Another early requisition was the *Roebuck*, one of the company's four Channel Islands ships called up (out of five, and the exception, *Ibex*, survived her own battle with the German Navy). The others were converted to minesweeping, and deployed to Scapa, where *Roebuck*, now renamed *Roedean*, met her end, mined in January 1915. She was the first railway ship casualty of the war, but one of her sisters, *Reindeer*, collided with and sank the Great Central's *Immingham* six months later, during the Dardanelles fiasco. At the end of the war, two ships of the Channel Islands fleet were to be found sailing the classically blue waters of the Aegean.

Rival to the GWR for the title of 'Premier Line', the London & North Western advertised its steamer services jointly with the Lancashire & Yorkshire, the Euston company losing no fewer than three of its handsome Irish Sea passenger ferries, two of them while in military service. The *Hibernia* had been renamed *Tara*, as there was a battleship already bearing Ireland's name, but it was the railway steamer which was torpedoed by a submarine in the Mediterranean in November 1915. *Tara* returned fire unsuccessfully and the U-boat captain generously towed the ships' lifeboats towards the Egyptian shore. The crew's ordeal was not over, unfortunately, as they were taken prisoner by nomads and force-marched through the desert, only being released some four months later when discovered by chance by a British Army unit. Sadly, eleven of the crew had lost their lives, the survivors being accorded a hero's welcome when returning to their native Anglesey.

Ten days later after the loss of the *Tara*, another of the L&NWR's Irish Sea ferries was lost. This was the *Anglia*, operating in the English Channel as a hospital ship, when she struck a mine within a mile of Folkestone. There was major loss of life, made worse by another vessel also striking a mine and sinking while attempting a rescue. King George V was particularly appalled by this tragedy, having sailed on the *Anglia* only three weeks previously. A final setback for the company was the loss of the ferry *Slieve Bloom*, sunk in a night collision with an American destroyer when operating without lights in the Irish Sea in March 1918.

Working closely with the L&NWR on Irish passenger sailings, the Lancashire & Yorkshire devoted more shipping capacity to cargo than the larger company. (And Edwin Pratt, in his book on Britain's railways at war, devotes more space to the Lancs & Yorks' marine operations than its railway activities.) The company operated out of Goole on the east coast as well as Fleetwood on the west, and four of those operating on the passage into German waters were arrested when the British Government's bungling declaration of war was made. Two ships escaped and a third was later released, but one, the *Dearne*, was seized, and was used by the Germans for minesweeping. Unusually, her end came when she was scuttled in the North Sea in December 1915, possibly after being challenged.

But the pride of the line were the 'Duke' turbine steamers on the passages to Belfast and Londonderry. Two of these, among the largest ferries in British waters, were requisitioned in October 1914, and one, *Duke of Albany*, was lost in August 1916, torpedoed in the North Sea when voyaging unescorted. Additionally, two of the company's smaller ships found Newhaven to be a dangerous port of departure, the *Rye* and the *Unity* both being torpedoed when working out of the Sussex port in 1918 within six weeks of each other, and in the same year when the LB&SCR's *Anjou* was accounted for here. By the end of the war, the company had awarded gold watches to two of its captains whose ships had escaped from U-boat attacks, while another earned a gratuity of £100 for damaging an enemy submarine. If this was accomplished by ramming, then a ship repair bill would have been inevitable.

Rivalling the North Western's Irish Sea steamers for elegance, the Midland had its own vessels operating out of Heysham, near Morecambe, to Northern Ireland ports and, in summer, to and from the Isle of Man. Five of the company's seven ships were requisitioned, but one failed to return to its owners. This was the *Donegal*, torpedoed when operating as a hospital ship crossing the Channel in April 1917. Eighty lives were lost, but most of the patients survived (610 according to official figures, out of 639), the crew and medical staff putting the safety of their charges above their own, a repeatedly awe inspiring feature of such sinkings. Besides Heysham, the Midland had an interest in the Stranraer–Larne crossing. Originally owning a quarter share in one of the companies on the landward side of Stranraer (the Portpatrick & Wigtownshire Joint), the Derby company increased its holdings when it enlarged its rail interests in the north of Ireland, becoming the largest constituent of the ferry company by the time of the First World War. Two of its ships were requisitioned in the conflict, and none of the fleet was lost.

Although it was the smallest pre-Grouping company owning ships, the Furness Railway operated both at sea and on freshwater. Its paddle steamers sailed out of Barrow, mainly to Fleetwood, the Isle of Man and Belfast. Two of them served gallantly at Dunkirk in 1940, when under non-railway ownership, both failing to return to port. The Furness company also operated tugs in the Barrow area, as well as pleasure vessels on Lakes Coniston and Windermere. One of those on the latter waterway, the *Tern*, dates from 1891, and is still in service. Although converted to diesel, this vessel represents a unique legacy from a company operating more than a century ago.

The three Scottish railway companies operating ships were the Caledonian, Glasgow & South Western, and the North British. The first of these owned the most impressive fleet, almost exclusively comprising paddle steamers on the Clyde. Two of these were lost to mines, one in the North Sea, one in the Channel. Rivalling this was the G&SW, with nine paddle vessels and a turbine-driven steamer. Two of these ships were lost, while the little paddler *Mercury* survived the war despite being damaged by mine twice, on the second occasion only twenty-four hours after returning from repairs caused by the previous explosion! The North British operated on the Forth as well as the Clyde, losing only one ship – to a North Sea mine – in the war, but had two of its paddle steamers destroyed by British forces in the White Sea in 1919 to avoid their falling into Bolshevik (i.e. Communist) hands.

The seaward contribution of the North Eastern Railway is more complicated to relate, as the York-based company followed a policy of buying interests in commercial shipping lines, and no conscious attempt was made to build a marine branch of the company with a monopoly of rail services in its part of the UK. This might seem a logical approach for a terrestrial transport concern – the largest dock-owning railway in the UK – to take towards marine matters, and the number of the area's vessels in use trading with neutral Scandinavia, and those involved in coal export, meant there was less naval requisitioning here. But the North Eastern's range of maritime services should not be underestimated – its advertisements in 1910 listed nine from the Tyne, six from West Hartlepool and Middlesbrough and a further six from Hull.

Despite not operating ships under its own flag, the NER made a major contribution to the work of the Admiralty, with its former AGM, Sir Eric Geddes following his successful work in streamlining Army communications on the Continent, with his appointment to the Cabinet as First Lord of the Admiralty. Once there he introduced a former NER goods official, George (later, Sir George) Beharrell, to undertake statistical research on the benefits of the belated convoy policy, and he was able to show that between August and October 1917 an escorted ship was seven times more likely to survive a voyage than a ship proceeding alone. This confirmed the wisdom of the convoy policy, one which the Admiralty had been reluctant to adopt, and saved many a merchant ship later in the war.

Like the Lancashire & Yorkshire, the Great Central, as mentioned earlier, was caught with three of its vessels in the Baltic in the first week of August 1914. These were the *City of Leeds*, *City of Bradford*, and the *Bury*, all of which attempted to clear German waters before the expiry of Britain's ultimatum. It is perhaps doubtful if they would have escaped anyway, but were not helped by confusion over the time specified in the ultimatum, the British Government apparently forgetting about the time difference. The ultimatum was intended to become effective at midnight, that is, midnight in London, but obviously one hour later in Germany. The crews, totalling eighty-nine, were interned in a prison camp for the entire war, although three female stewardesses were freed. But the captain of the *Bury* died during the long years of imprisonment, as did two of his crewmen. The three vessels were returned to the company in November 1918, and the *Bury*, while later owned by the LNER, went on to a distinguished career in the next war, escorting Atlantic convoys. In one twenty-four hour period, the crew of the *Bury* rescued 170 seamen from torpedoed ships, earning six military honours.

The GCR was badly affected by the war, and not only with the enforced absence of the three ships mentioned above. Since much of its trade from Grimsby was conducted with Baltic ports, the company was hardly able to resist other calls on its vessels. A number served with the Navy, the modern freighter *Immingham* being lost, as previously mentioned, (and surprisingly omitted from the official volume, *Statistics of the Military Effort of the British Empire during the Great War*, which carries a named list of civilian vessels lost in service of the military). The hard-pressed Great Eastern was glad to hire GCR vessels, and perhaps not surprisingly, it was a Great Central ship, the *Marylebone* flying GER colours, which was the first into Antwerp after the war. The company's last ship to be lost was the *Wrexham*, wrecked after striking an uncharted rock in the White Sea, far from her regular routes.

Two of the company's humbler vessels played an interesting role in the war. The ferries *Brocklesby* and *Killingholme* normally operated between Hull and New Holland, but in February 1916 were requisitioned by the Admiralty and became the Navy's only aircraft carriers driven by paddle wheel. As seaplane carriers they were regarded as unsuccessful, and they would appear to be a strange choice for such a role, being too slow for fleet work and with limited fuel capacity. Both returned safely to civilian duties, being taken over by the LNER, and *Killingholme* served in the next war as a barrage balloon carrier.

By returning to the Thames, we come last to the Great Eastern, and this company had the dubious distinction of learning that two of its employees had been tried for murder by a German court, and one was shot at dawn. He was Captain Charles Fryatt, master of the GER steamer *Brussels* which was taken in prize by enemy vessels in the North Sea in June 1916. Captain Fryatt had become something of a marked man following an earlier exchange with German forces, where he had attempted to ram a U-boat after apparently surrendering to it. This followed unrealistic, indeed absurd, advice from First Lord of the Admiralty Winston Churchill that civilian ships, menaced by a surfaced enemy submarine, should attempt to sink it by ramming, despite their lack of a reinforced bow.

On this fateful occasion in 1916, it appears that the Germans believed that the GER employee had previously abused truce conditions, and following a 'trial' of both Captain Fryatt and his Chief Engineer, the former was sentenced to death. After this inhumane deed had been carried out, described by Edwin Pratt as 'judicial murder', the body was returned to Britain. Even the mild-mannered Prime Minister Herbert Asquith was roused to declare that Germany would be held to account, and the murdered civilian was given a hero's funeral. In passing, one is forced to wonder what was the point of Britain boasting a magnificent and unchallengeable battle fleet when German destroyers were perfectly capable of capturing or sinking unescorted British vessels just a few miles offshore. The release of more British cruisers and destroyers to escort duties, with naval airships and aircraft taking over reconnoitring surveys for the Grand Fleet, would surely have been preferable.

The Great Eastern was ill-treated by the Admiralty. Despite losing so many of its ships for stores transport and minesweeping, it was required to run an increased service across the North Sea, but without any kind of escort protection before the autumn of 1916. Even then, the company's *Colchester* was taken by the enemy, when two RN destroyers failed to escort it properly, in a manner that was frankly negligent. While no one lost their lives on this occasion, a railway crew and passengers spent more than two years interned.

Underwriting the seriousness of GER ships sailing without protection, one historian (David Stevenson) has speculated that an intercepted intelligence message from an agent travelling on the Harwich–Hook of Holland passage may have led to the exposure of an Allied spy network operating in the Netherlands. (Their intelligence was based on train-watching, when observation of rail traffic could reveal the enemy's intentions, as happened just before the German assault in Champagne in June 1917.) Stevenson argues that this network lost ninety-eight agents executed and 644 imprisoned; many of them after the interrogation of a Great Eastern Railway passenger. Not that the company was in any way to blame – although its directors might have made a greater agitation to require the Royal Navy to prove it could still rule the waves.

***

In retrospect, it seems incredible that British *railway* employees would find themselves in a German prison camp, or being force-marched through the North African desert for weeks on end, or worst of all, facing a firing squad. These were three of the extreme fates which befell the crews of railway steamers, but their actual lives on board were no less dangerous. Railway ships operated anywhere in the northern hemisphere, from the warm waters of the Aegean to the freezing coastline of Russia, then in the grip of civil war. Their underpaid crews had to cope with mines, attacks from warships and unseen submarines, while a number of vessels were lost because of collisions with other Allied vessels operating in poor visibility conditions, and without lights. It is an extraordinary record of gallantry, inspiration, and unselfish determination.

Letter from the Somme

Effects on Traffic

Late in 1916, General Sir Douglas Haig invited the general managers on the REC main committee to visit the Somme battlefield to see conditions for themselves.

This was an extraordinary request, with British troops engaged in the worst bloodbath the Army had ever experienced. Fortunately, the battle had ended, in the usual stalemate, by the time the delegation arrived on 9 December, and Edwin Pratt, in describing this visit (not led by Herbert Walker, who was unwell), appeared to believe that Haig was asking for tracks 'across the destroyed zone' and no doubt onward to Berlin. In fact Haig was being pressured by his French allies to take more responsibility for his own transport arrangements behind the lines. The Nord company had lost nearly half its mileage to the German invader, but found that its remaining network was carrying twice as much traffic as before, while both the Est and PLM companies faced doubled traffic demand. 'The intensity with which fighting has developed,' Haig announced 'necessitates enormous extension of broad [standard] and 60-cm gauge railways … in advance of railhead, to which point the French have heretofore done the working.' So Britain's railway companies were not alone in encountering increased traffic demand and logistical difficulties – so had the French. But it was back to 'Blighty's railways' for a solution. 'I need very large supplies of railway material, rolling stock, locomotives and personnel,' Haig stated baldly.

Interestingly, Haig was addressing the REC, in contrast to the Admiralty, who had ignored it. And the response was immediate. The official statistical digest issued three years after the war's end (see list of sources) shows that 1,268 locomotives were supplied to the Army in France (and not including ROD units) by December 1918. Even excluding those moved to Egypt and Mesopotamia, this is 6 per cent of the total operating in the UK at arguably the busiest time in the railways' history, when something like 20 per cent of British locomotives awaited repair (as the Cabinet was informed in May of that year). The most transported to France in a single month were 165 in March 1917, only three months after Haig made his appeal. There were 53,371 British-owned wagons on French railways by the end of the war, the most transported in a single month being 4,651 in, again, March 1917 (and this included GSA rolling stock). Making this all the more remarkable was the lack of train ferries before the end of that year. Three were available from then on at Richborough, with a fourth at Southampton by the end of the war.

From 2 January 1917, the companies had responded in two ways – retraction and supply. Around 170 miles of new track was laid by the British Army in France in 1918, and in order to provide such basic equipment as track panels, points, and crossings, there had to be a wholesale programme of closures, both of branch lines and wayside stations, accompanied by a 50 per cent increase in fares, to discourage passengers. Having hastened in this effort to supply Haig with the equipment he needed – a change from his constantly repeated demand for more infantry (or 'cannon-fodder', as Siegfried Sassoon called foot soldiers) – a belt-tightening exercise began on Britain's railways, which, it could be argued, would never be relaxed. Such charming locales as Port Carlisle on the Solway Firth would lose its passenger trains, while services in and out of London's busiest termini would be cut by one-third. Some lines were singled, some vanished altogether. The L&NWR alone withdrew services from forty-six stations, the NBR from fifty-nine, and the Great Western closed six branch lines completely.

* * *

The changes being undertaken were announced at the end of 1916 by the Board of Trade (of which the REC was of course a part), and the enabling legislation quoted was not the 1871 Act, but DORA. This was the Defence of the Realm Act hurriedly passed in 1914, and there were ten resulting measures on Britain's railways dating from the second day of 1917.

A general curtailment of passenger services offered, through timetable reduction and station closures.

No seat reservations for individuals or parties.

'Curtailment' of sleeping services and dining cars.

Withdrawal of 'slip' coach services (where an intermediate station would be served by a coach being detached while an express train was in motion, and the carriage being braked to a stop by the guard).

No transport of road vehicles by train.

A 50 per cent increase in passenger fares, but the initial announcement excluded workmen's, traders', and 'zone' tickets, while also appearing to do so for season tickets, which were arguably too cheap already.

No fare reductions to be permitted, except in special cases.

Guaranteed 'through' ticketing, where more than one company involved.

A 100 lb luggage limit – probably a blessing as passengers could not always expect the assistance of station porters.

All this could be seen as an indictment of the REC's casual treatment of war at its outbreak, particularly in allowing holiday excursion fares and continued luxury on long-distance expresses. The wording of this measure announced in December 1916 was not exactly clear cut in regard to season tickets, and subsequent Government policy was no less confusing. In May 1918 a regulation was issued under DORA to the effect that 'no railway shall be obliged to issue season tickets' and went on to decree that within 12 miles of Charing Cross, applicants might be questioned and be asked to justify, in writing, their reasons for wishing to travel twice daily on the railway. Presumably this was to ensure that SECR stations were left free for military travellers and cargoes, but Edwin Pratt believed that season tickets were too much of a good thing for travellers anyway. Nevertheless it does appear something of a penalty on a railway company which was serving the military establishment so loyally, and where other travel limitations, on off-peak travel for example, could have been found.

The restriction of restaurant cars was no more than minimal, and certainly not a complete ban, at a time when long-distance trains were taking so much longer on their journeys. In July 1914 Britain's railways had operated 474 restaurant and 'tea' cars – the latter the equivalent of later 'buffet' cars – along with Pullman vehicles, but by the month of the armistice, November 1918, the total was seventy-two. It rose to 284 by the following August, the first such month in peacetime in five years. In the depths of the war the only companies offering on-board catering were the Midland and LBSC (twenty vehicles each), London & South Western (twelve), Great Central and Great Northern of Ireland (eight), Great Eastern (four), and two on the Glasgow & South Western. The absence of catering on the east and west coast companies, with London to Aberdeen routes of more than 520 miles each, and schedules now exceeding thirteen hours, is a surprise.

The last of the strictures listed above – the limitation on passenger luggage – produced an unexpected response. While women had now undertaken many portering duties at stations, and some seemed not inconvenienced in the least by heavy cases, the authorities were nevertheless made aware of a problem resulting from weight limitations. REC Circular 941 announced in May 1917 that special permits would be issued to travellers who were 'experts attached to certain Government Departments [who] experience difficulty in carrying out their experiments' presumably because such 'boffins' were unhappy about being prevented from carrying or supervising their own scientific equipment and seeing it being thrown into the guard's van. Acting Chairman (by now, Sir) Herbert Walker stressed, however, that any such permits had to be signed by him personally.

A summary follows of how the companies responded to Haig's entreaty in the first month of 1917. Nearly of all these service retractions were to be restored in 1919, but the wisdom, or otherwise, of railway companies' sacrifices being made in terms of closures is discussed later.

* * *

The SE&CR, always a line serving passengers in the form of Continental travellers, resort holidaymakers, and Kent commuters, found itself having to reduce its passenger services from January 1917. Daily traffic into and out of its London stations was lowered from 436 daily to 280. Five branches had lost their services before the end of 1916, and now another five followed, with additional Sunday closures at such varied locations as London's Cannon Street and the venerable Canterbury & Whitstable branch. As a result of all this, forty-seven passenger guards were 'released', twelve of them to the forces, and the rest to goods duties. These economies allowed the closure of some thirteen signal boxes, at a time when it was decided to allow eighteen-year-olds to serve in boxes, lowering the existing age limit from twenty. (As already related, the South Eastern was finding the Woolwich Arsenal a powerful magnet for labour.) Coal carried on the system increased from approximately 94,500 tons to 146,500 in 1915–16, a rise of more than 50 per cent, while the enormous increase in munitions traffic in the Woolwich area has already been mentioned. This calendar year would also see the full commissioning of a military harbour at Richborough, reached over the company's metals and involving the use of a train ferry for the first time in decades. (More details have been given on this under 'Canals'.) A pleasant exception to all this vigorous austerity came with the May 1917 renewal of reduced fares for fruit pickers – a matter of particular interest to the South Eastern, and a source of pocket money for city children.

The LBSCR continued to be affected by the vastly increased demand for war material, having been heavily involved in support operations at Newhaven from the first week of war. Its near-disasters involving explosive cargoes in 1917–18 show that military demands were ever present. Newhaven harbour was owned by a separate company, in which the 'Brighton' had an interest, but was operated by the railway, with 2,500 staff employed there initially. Some 500 women workers were brought in as the war went on. The Brighton line had already to decline an Army request for 0-6-0 tender goods engines, offering a number of 0-6-2 tank locomotives instead, an offer not recorded by Edwin Pratt. As one of the smaller companies in terms of mileage – and not originally asked to nominate its General Manager to the REC's supreme committee – it was not expected to make the same contribution in terms of track supplies or vehicles.

Just along the coast, the South Western, which described itself as 'The Military Line', provided fifty 0-6-0s, of which thirty-six went to France, nine to Mesopotamia, and five to Salonika, but also sent 12 miles of track, after closing and lifting the Basingstoke–Alton line. It also managed Southampton Docks, and the importance of this utility can be gauged from the figures of troop numbers passing through – 7.13 million travelling out, but only 4.8 million returning. This is not as morbid a statistic as it may appear, as there was an increasing tendency to send troops to the nearer Continental ports as the relative position of the warring armies became clearer.

At York, the North Eastern responded to the call by supplying 27 miles of track, and was already in the process of lending fifty locomotives and 4,547 wagons, plus two steam-powered cranes. Its military contribution in the form of a Pioneers battalion was a major commitment, and there was also the loss of one of the company's tugs, the *Stranton* (HMS *Char*), tragically involving the supreme sacrifice from the entire crew, eight of them NER employees.

The Midland's response was to close two stations and their line between Bennerley Junction and Kimberley in the Nottingham area, 'freeing' 28 miles of track, and singling another 25 miles from double. Seventy-eight locomotives were loaned, along with no fewer than 6,000 wagons and fifty brake vans. This must have stretched the company's carrying resources considerably – the Midland's coal traffic into London had risen 71 per cent from 1914 by this time, with a maximum of eighty coal trains in a single day.

Its rival, the London & North Western, loaned the largest number of locomotives – 111 – of which ninety-eight went to France and the remainder to Egypt. Of 6,370 wagons loaned, fifteen were lost at sea. Some 56 miles of track was supplied and no fewer than forty-six stations closed, the highest number in England. Track mileage was in addition to the supply of 30,000 sleepers, and the total included no fewer than six cranes, one a 36-ton-capacity breakdown vehicle. The part played by Crewe and Wolverton works in supplying ambulance trains has already been described.

The 'Lancs & Yorks' was soon to merge with the L&NWR, and its main contribution to the war effort was at sea. As described in the relevant chapter, the L&Y was the only English company operating from both east and west coasts, although it had to close down its North Sea operations immediately when war was declared, indeed, even earlier in the case of the Goole–Hamburg run. A number of goods 0-6-0s were loaned to the Army, while the company's works manufactured a considerable amount of material for 60-cm narrow-gauge transport, in addition to road motor vehicles.

Rivalling the L&NWR for the title of 'Premier Line', the Great Western certainly compared with its northern counterpart in supplying the Army's needs. The ninety-five locomotives loaned were accompanied by 105 tenders, the 49 miles of track by no fewer than 50,000 sleepers. As mentioned earlier, the military also seem to have made off with fifty of the company's valuable draught horses, without troubling to pay for them! Routes and stations closed included six complete branch lines – Alcester–Bearley, Titley–Eardisley, Moorswater–Caradon, Monmouth–Coleford, Uxbridge (High Street)–Denham, Bridport (East Street)–West Bay – and thirty stations in all.

On the eastern side of the country, the Great Northern loaned twenty-six 0-6-0s with condensing gear designed by Nigel Gresley to reduce visible exhaust, and, in theory, to allow working into danger areas. Its tank engines powered the previously described armoured train assembled at Crewe. The Great Eastern provided forty-three goods engines on loan, assorted wagons, and 30,000 sleepers, 22,000 of which were previously unused. Meanwhile, the Great Central had supplied the 'template' for the ubiquitous war locomotive, the equivalent of the Austerity classes of the Second World War, the Robinson 2-8-0. Apart from the 521 ordered by the Railway Operating Department, their 'foster parent' company, the GCR loaned six new 2-8-0s of its own in addition to thirty-three smaller goods engines. 3,267 wagons were supplied for use in France and thirty-five brake vans for Egypt. Two complete ten-coach passenger trains were supplied for use as leave specials. These would be for officers of course – the other ranks might have had a rest and recreation behind the lines from time to time, but they would not see 'Blighty' again unless wounded, or until the war was over.

In Scotland, the Caledonian closed forty-seven stations, the North British fifty-nine (although the latter did open a new stopping place, called Rosyth Halt, on the Edinburgh–Perth line, obviously serving what was soon to become the successor base to Scapa Flow for capital ships). A surprisingly high proportion of station closures took place in Edinburgh and Glasgow, conforming to the theory that cuts were being made which would still leave the public with alternative transport facilities. Both companies supplied 0-6-0s for work in France, one of the Caledonian's being observed at Cologne in 1919. Those of the NBR later bore the names of some of the commanders whose reputations were still unsullied. Ironically, one of these engines, commemorating the Battle of Mons, was still working as late as the mid-1960s.

For its part, the G&SWR supplied the equivalent of 5 miles of track, including 15,000 new sleepers, 100 points, and pre-engineered crossings. Among necessary closures was the Catrine branch, opened only twelve years earlier. Meanwhile, the Highland was not expected to lend or supply material – it had enough problems of its own – and had been loaned locomotives and rolling stock from a number of companies: Caledonian, G&SWR (although the restricted loading gauge would have to be borne in mind) and the SE&CR. The Admiralty operated five ex-LB&SCR tanks on the Inverness Harbour and Invergordon branches.

Equipment loaned to BEF in response to Haig's request, Dec. 1916. (Summary only)

Company	Locomotives	Wagons	Track (Miles)	Other
Midland	78	6,000	53	50 brake vans
L&NWR	111	6,370	56	6 cranes
North Eastern	50	4,547	27	2 steam cranes
Great Western	95	6,567	49	238 carriages
Great Central	39	3,267	–	2 'leave' trains
L&SWR	50		12	

Source: Pratt (see bibliography). This listing of company loans to the Army does not imply competition. Those companies not lending any substantial amount, but contributing in other ways, are discussed in the text. Not all the locomotive loans are recorded by Pratt – e.g. those of the CR, LBSCR and NBR.

* * *

Before leaving January 1917 to look farther ahead, we must consider the two other important announcements made in that month which affected Britain's railways. Ireland was, of course, still part of the United Kingdom in that year, but the bloodily suppressed Easter Rising had taken place in April 1916, and front-line troops were having to be transferred across both the Channel and the Irish Sea. It was now thought necessary to bring Irish railways under Government control and they were taken over from 1 January 1917, with, again, the 1871 Regulation of the Forces Act as the enabling legislation. Chairman of the Irish Railway Executive Committee was a senior civil servant, Sir William Byrne, but the Acting Chairman was E. A. Neale, General Manager of the Dublin-based Great Southern & Western Railway. Interestingly, the Irish 'secretary company' to the Army's Irish Command had been the Belfast-based Great Northern Railway of Ireland, although not represented on Great Britain's REC. By the following year, the IREC was to impose a 50 per cent increase in passenger fares, in line with Great Britain's.

Another measure carried out in January 1917 concerned control of goods wagons' movements. To assist the Railway Clearing House, now facing an intensified level of traffic, it was decided to 'group' railways into twelve entities, based on the major companies, with unaffiliated lines being considered as part of that geographical area – the North Sunderland was considered in the North Eastern group, for example. The groups comprised the eleven members of the REC GM's committee in 1916, plus the Scottish companies considered as a single entity. 'At each junction where traffic is exchanged a record is kept of all loaded and empty wagons which are exchanged,' as Edwin Pratt explained. This was a formalisation of what was being done already by the RCH, but clearly the matter had now increased in importance in view of the increase in goods traffic and in particular the unprecedented transport of coal over hundreds of miles. His Majesty's enemies doubtless needed no such auditing measures on their nationalised systems.

As a result of Haig's appeal, many communities found themselves with no rail service, although only in locations 'where the public could be served by tramways or by motor omnibuses'. Service withdrawal was intended to be temporary, and almost all lines were reopened in 1919, but needless to say, this was to invite rival transport operations to fill the vacuum, for the movement of both goods and people. Railways' future problems may have sprung from this, and their managements were slow to learn – and this still applies today – that even diversions and temporary withdrawals will simply cause the public to look elsewhere for their transport options.

* * *

On a more positive note, in 1917 the Association of Railway Locomotive Engineers (ARLE) – which at one time had been little more than a social club for CMEs – began issuing technical guidelines to the railway industry. As if to underline its enhanced status, ARLE was asked by Government to consider designing an array of standardised locomotives for general service. Chaired by G. J. Churchward of the GWR, the association began the preparation of drawings for classes of 2-8-0s, 4-6-0s, and (perhaps surprisingly) 4-4-0s, but with priority for a mixed-traffic 2-6-0. Early in 1918 it was decided that twelve classes in the above wheel arrangements would meet national requirements, a number curiously adjacent to the introduction of eleven 'Standard' classes on nationalised British Railways in 1951.

One locomotive designer supporting the work of the association, but not enthusiastic about the standardisation plan was the Great Northern's Nigel Gresley. His assistant A. V. Bulleid was later quoted by author E. S. Cox as saying that Gresley would never agree to 'a railway crawling with engines designed by others'. Specifically, Gresley believed that a standardisation scheme would result in an increase in the number of spare parts having to be stored in addition to those required for existing rolling stock. This might be true for a transitional period, but with companies facing the need for repair and reconstruction – and even as late as October 1918 there was no guarantee that the war would end in the foreseeable future – his misgivings should not have been regarded as insurmountable. But the war did cease in the late autumn of that year, and brought this interesting scheme to an end.

* * *

We have seen the effect of the railways' generous support of Haig and his Army, resulting in service withdrawals and closures. But what of the effect on existing services, those too important to remove from the timetable?

By the final year of the war, a passenger travelling from London to Birmingham could spend a minimum of an extra half-hour on such a comparatively short journey. For the journey to and from Euston by L&NWR, two hours and thirty-five minutes were required, an addition of 29 per cent, and although the Great Western could cut five minutes from that, the journey from Paddington still required half an hour longer than in 1914. At the other end of the scale, King's Cross–Aberdeen took no less than thirteen and a half hours, a 22 per cent increase on the previous schedule of just over eleven. London–Edinburgh had not been 'express' for some twenty years, thanks to the 1896 cartel designed to slow down express services (see this author's *London's Scottish Railways*), but was now nearly an additional two hours slower, an average speed of no more than 40 mph. Paddington–Plymouth was fifty-three minutes longer than before, while it took nearly six hours from Waterloo, a 20 per cent increase in journey time – and dining cars had almost all been withdrawn.

In *Regeneration*, Pat Barker's absorbing novel concerning the treatment of Army officers recovering from shell shock, she has the poet Robert Graves complaining that his train from Liverpool to Edinburgh had 'stopped at every station'. While this was an exaggeration compounded by artistic licence, it shows good research by the novelist. The easiest way for timetablers to lengthen journey times was to introduce more intermediate stops, compensating for any reduction in stopping services.

Allotments

If, at the outset of war, jingoistic crowds had been told that they would come close to starvation because of enemy submarines, they would never have believed it. But as the war went on, agriculture had to revolutionise its working practices to ensure the production of enough food for the nation. Not surprisingly, the railway companies realised that they possessed sizable land banks which had no immediate operational use and could be converted to allotments. Already such companies as the GWR and NER were each providing space for some 7,000 allotments, but by the end of the war, the land 'allotted' by railways could have equated to approximately 125 square miles. In comparison, England's smallest county at the time, Rutland, had an area of 147 square miles.

In his history of the railways' war, Edwin Pratt specifies that the Great Eastern and Great Western companies offered allotments only to staff, but all would have given priority to employees or their families anyway. The Great Western made available space for an extra 13,059 allotments, in addition to the 7,653 already provided. From December 1916, GWR staff would pay an annual rent of 3*d* or 4*d* 'per rod or perch' (archaic measurements of area) depending on location if the land had been cultivated previously, but would pay nothing if it was pristine. The North Eastern came second in such provision, with some 10,000 new plots in addition to the existing 6,969. The London & North Western provided space for some 14,000 altogether, with the Midland's provision standing at 9,500 over some 752 acres. More than 7,000 plots were provided by the London & South Western, although neither the LB&SCR nor SE&CR features in Pratt's survey. 5,000 sites were 'allotted' by the Great Eastern, while the Caledonian and Great Central both exceeded 4,000.

Fruit and vegetables from allotments were not the only foodstuffs which the railways were expected to produce from their own resources. From May 1916, the REC was asked by the War Office Forage Committee to ensure that as much hay as possible should be produced from the railways' own cuttings and embankments. The committee's Colonel Morgan conceded that railway-grown hay 'would not be of the first quality but quite suitable as "chaffing", of which all companies, I think, use a large proportion'. There was no suggestion in the REC Circular 563 that chaff could be sold or redistributed by the companies, although it must be said that their horse ownership was of course greatly reduced at this time, possibly leaving a surplus.

Demobilisation

Following the armistice of November 1918, 'demob happy' was not a term likely to be applied to members of Britain's fighting forces. Having assembled the world's greatest Navy, and the largest ever Army in the nation's history, the UK was faced by a huge logistical challenge in standing down men who had, in many cases, been away from home for years, to say nothing of the potential consequences of the horror and despair that many of them must have experienced during active service.

But the authorities had to be ever mindful of the fact that Germany and her allies had asked only for a ceasefire, with their borders remaining intact up until that time. In theory, the machines of war were still ticking over, although there was a sense of exhaustion which was almost palpable, particularly from the former enemy. The so-called Peace Conference was established at Versailles in 1919, developing into a confabulation of presidents and prime ministers all trying to impose their own ideas on the newly acclaimed peace and, in the case of the European allies, exact maximum territorial and financial penalties on Germany. During the resulting delay, soldiers who expected an immediate return home found themselves in barracks and holding camps, resulting in near-mutinies, and in the case of the French, desertion on a major scale.

Britain's Royal Navy would experience mutinies within a few years, but from a different cause – pay cuts – and the impatience that so many sailors must have felt in late 1918 was alleviated by generous leave conditions (certainly in comparison with the Army) of twelve days over the festive season. In particular, crews in the Grand Fleet received a welcome opportunity to visit home, with the North British, North Eastern, and Midland railways being asked to supply transport to take the crews southwards. This was no easy task as Rosyth – now succeeding Scapa Flow as home to the Grand Fleet – was accessed only by a steep NBR branch from the Edinburgh–Aberdeen main line, facing northwards, and the Port Edgar branch on the southern shore of the Firth was equally steeply graded.

The logistics of all this were considerable. The core of the fleet at this time were twenty-two battleships, supplemented by the newer oil-fuelled Queen Elizabeth class, as well as battlecruisers, cruisers, and destroyers, the last named being based at Port Edgar. With an average battleship having a crew of around 900, the number of men to be moved would number up to 60,000, the equivalent of the original BEF, and all required to be taken southwards and then brought back again within a fortnight. Sensibly, the RN 'pre-sorted', as it were, the men into destinations before taking them off the ships in relays. This enabled the NBR to transport up to 14,000 in twenty-two trains per day. From Edinburgh, the ECML and Waverley Routes were utilised, with the North Eastern taking over at Berwick and the Midland and L&NWR at Carlisle. This successful operation was later acknowledged with gratitude by Admiral Sir David Beattie, a man not believed to be easily pleased.

When it came to final demobilisation, the Royal Navy dispersed crews when ships were decommissioned or reduced to reserve, with men being released at such bases as Chatham and Devonport. In the first quarter of 1919, up to 3,900 men were sent daily from these bases London-wards in leave trains, the records showing an average of 265 sailors per train. This was almost as comfortable a ratio of passenger to available accommodation as when the BEF was taken to Southampton in August 1914.

* * *

The Army took longer to release men, attempting to do so initially on the 'first in, first out' principle. This rapidly became contentious, with employers such as the railway companies expecting the return of workers who should arguably not have been drafted in the first place, and who were required as the railways found themselves having to devise yet more new traffic streams. We have already seen that the REC had requested – in vain – the return of former railwaymen unsuitable for foreign service, but even with the arrival of peace, this was still a matter of negotiation. Sir Sam Fay, the Great Central's General Manager who served with the Ministry of War from 1916, wrote in March 1919 that – five months after the armistice, no less – he had attended a meeting where he 'managed to get some 9,000 more railway workers released'. Winston Churchill was in the chair on this occasion as War Minister, with Field Marshal Douglas Haig in attendance, their presence indicating the seriousness of the matter.

The official statistics show that just over 105,000 railwaymen returned to 'civvy street' within eighteen months of the armistice. In the same period 220,000 miners and 301,000 agricultural workers were demobilised, and it says much for those men who had stayed behind, and the women who took up so much men's labour, that the country had been able to win on the Home Front as well as on the continent and at sea. Of course, the 'demob' of technically valuable personnel ahead of, say, 'Old Contemptibles' could only be a source of dismay and anger to many.

As with men, so it was with horses. At the end of the war it was intended that 125,000 of them should be returned to 'Blighty' when it became clear that Germany was in no mood to reignite the conflict. In his recent history of the war, Jeremy Paxman writes of British officers attempting to buy their, or their battalions', horses to spare them from the Continental meat markets, but there was in fact an elaborate programme in place for the transport of draught animals back to four ports in Britain: Southampton, Tilbury, London (Surrey Docks), and Hull. They would be quarantined for two weeks at one of these ports before being sent on to one of fourteen regional centres for sale. (The Army presumably regarded itself as undisputed owner of the animals, no matter how they had been obtained!)

In practice, the schedule became scrambled as the French authorities requested a faster removal of British horses, and even the Richborough train ferry was pressed into service to take 400 at a time in livestock wagons shuttling across the Channel from Calais. The Army then found that horses could fetch a higher price in some parts of the country than in others, and the fourteen-centre plan seems to have slipped somewhat. Purchasers added to the problems by requesting individual rail horse boxes, for which there was 'abnormal demand'. The railways themselves became purchasers, the archives of one pre-Grouping company recording the purchase of 'a handsome grey Percheron', and its new owners would never be likely to forget its service in war 'numerous signs of which it still bears on its body'. Pleasant to relate, the company later won an animal welfare award for its care of this particular horse.

Recognition

At least Haig showed an awareness of what railways had done to help achieve final victory, unlike some historians. In a letter to the South Eastern & Chatham Railway on 23 December 1918, he wrote, 'Track has been torn up to give us rails; engines, trucks, men, capable operating staff etc., all have been sent abroad to us, regardless of the special needs and demands of the people at Home, and without any hesitation.'

He might have acknowledged that company's contribution in the form of supplying ships capable of taking part in fleet operations as well as everyday ferrying, but he was of course a land commander, and may have been unaware of the scale of the railways' maritime contribution, as indeed so many have been.

Any reader studying the progress of Haig's command on the Western Front would realise the significance of how Britain's railways responded to his letter from the Somme. Haig spent much of his time dealing with politicians, both British and French, as well as working with Allied generals – French, Belgian, American, even Portuguese – to say nothing of trying to second-guess where the next enemy attack would come from, or where his own Army should strike next. Haig has been described as a notorious intriguer, as his wife's position at the royal court allowed him considerable leverage against elected politicians, and his own commander in 1914–15, Sir John French, was in financial thrall to him. But Haig was a man of few words. A quick and effective response to his request for assistance from the REC must have impressed him.

To lose rail services to allow the Army more trackage overseas is a form of sacrifice, yet this is a word hardly used lightly in terms of the First World War. In the next section, the railways' staff contribution is considered in terms of casualties, in a literal sense of the concept of 'sacrifice'. But without devaluing the word, it seems unarguable that it can also refer to the rail companies' unselfishness in the light of future competition. The retraction of railway services began in 1917, even if so many of them were restored within two years, and during this interregnum the public found other methods of transport. After the war the flood of surplus road vehicles – and of men able to operate and maintain them – was to send railways spiralling on a downward trajectory which would involve the Grouping, then more and permanent closures, then Nationalisation, then … Beeching.

The Cost

Railways in Belgium and northern France counted wartime costs in terms of physical devastation. British railways were by no means immune, but damage caused by bombs or bombardment were minor compared to their Continental counterparts. On the other hand, there were to be financial costs, even if these were not immediately pressing.

As shown in the following table, the gross revenue on the national network increased by 42 per cent between 1913 and the final year of war. But expenditure increased by 62 per cent, despite this being a time of service withdrawals and reductions, and a minimum of new investment. Wage increases were obviously responsible for this increase, despite the lower amounts paid to women workers. As a result, net income increased by only around 2 per cent when the network was at its busiest. The use of the 1913 net total when Government was considering railway finances in the next decade, was to prove unhelpful.

	Gross	Expenditure	Net
1913	139,253,000	87,242,000	52,011,000
1914	139,098,000	88,173,000	50,925,000
1918	197,293,000	143,342,000	53,925,000

The Government was effectively guaranteeing the railways against loss during the war, working from the net receipts collected in the first half of 1913. If the income for the corresponding period for the following year was less, the Government would compensate accordingly. There was some tweaking of the figures in the first nine months of the war, where it appears that Government was seeking to limit its commitment when costs began to rise steeply, but this was dropped in April 1915 when the railways undertook to pay a quarter of the sum of war bonuses newly awarded to railway staff.

But these 1913–18 figures were seminal, regarded as a benchmark for railway performance by successive governments, without taking into account changing social and industrial factors. The 1923 Grouping of Britain's railways was fostered by a general belief that the wartime measure of Government control was just as desirable in the subsequent years of peace. Even someone as conservative as Winston Churchill (although nominally a Liberal at the time) believed that the railways constituted an essential part of the nation's way of life – as they had proved in war – and should be nationalised. If this was politically unacceptable, the legislation of 1921, which established four super-companies, still carried a degree of supervision which continued Government influence, if not exactly control, beyond the dissolution of the Railway Executive Committee. A separate Act of 1919 had, of course, already set up a Ministry of Transport.

Also in January 1919, legislation addressed the question of hours worked, introducing the eight-hour day, much to Walker's fury. Describing the new measure as 'perhaps the most wicked thing that has ever been perpetrated on a community', Sir Herbert argued that a signalman on a branch line might spend the day under-employed, compared to, say, signalling staff at a busy junction. He did not appear to have considered that management could have tackled this over the years by increased automation or better working practices on lesser-used lines, or even by staff rotation. In other words, better management. Meanwhile, works staff were included in the forty-seven-hour week arrangement applied to engineering workers in other industries.

* * *

The 'par' measurements for financial performance did not come into effect until 1928, a full fifteen years after the model year to which the railways' turnover was being compared, and following a period of serious unrest in the coal industry, and an unprecedented general strike, to say nothing of the spiralling growth of the road industry. Not surprisingly, by the time the new rail companies launched on their 'par' courses in 1928, they found they were competing with twice as many motor vehicles as had been on the roads seven years previously, and proportionately even more compared with the yardstick year of 1913. The return of railwaymen from the services, displacing cheaper labour (i.e. women), would of course increase operating costs, and from this time on wages would become a major proportion of rail expenditure, particularly with working hours being restricted by legislation in 1919. But this was hardly an employees' bonanza – operating staff were still having to work long hours in practice, as railwaymen's reminiscences make only too clear.

* * *

It would certainly appear that the 62 per cent increase in expenditure, as an average figure, meant that several companies experienced an even greater rise. It should be no surprise that this would include the companies with the largest workforces, as wages were the single greatest area of increase, a rise triggered by food prices. This was inevitable as food importation was more difficult at a time of blockade by U-boat, but would have been much worse if there had been no reduction in rail services offered and less employment of cheap labour – in other words, women – although it should be recalled that more than half of male vacancies remained unfilled.

To summarise (and using approximate figures), the largest companies were inevitably among those which experienced the greatest percentage increase on their expenditure over the years 1915–18. The Great Eastern saw a rise of 63 per cent, the North Western 65, the Midland 67, and the Great Western 68. Interestingly, and somewhat disappointingly, the Great Northern and North Eastern – two companies which declined to offer a war bonus to female staff halfway through this sample period, saw a lesser rise in costs – 52 and 53 per cent respectively. To spoil the theory somewhat, the South Eastern, despite having less than a quarter of the GWR's mileage, saw a 69 per cent rise in expenditure, despite similarly refusing to increase the wages for its female workforce.

There should have been no winners or losers among the companies, in any event. One of the South Eastern's historians, David Gould, believed that by the end of the war the company 'was almost on its knees, because costs had gone up, yet receipts were still kept to the artificial level' – that is, the level of net profit gained in 1913 decided the amount paid by the Government. Mr Gould has praised this company not only for its efficiency in supporting the war effort, but for doing so without expecting its own enrichment. In his book on the South Eastern, David Gould describes it as 'the most important transport system in the Great War, because of its geographical position', but 'by the end it was almost on its knees'. As shown above, there appears to be evidence to support this claim. But Mr Gould raises an interesting point.

This was a commercial company restrained from profiting from its geographical position, one it had gained perfectly fairly and consolidated through good service to the travelling public. But because it was a railway service, it had to consider itself a national asset, being required to perform to the Government's will and rewarded at official discretion, with income from the increased traffic being 'pooled' with that from companies less heavily burdened. It would probably be undeniable that some of the smaller companies in rural areas would carry less war-related traffic, particularly early in the conflict before the spread of ROFs, and the movement of troops travelling to and from remote training centres or convalescent hospitals. In other words the South Eastern could not benefit either from its location or its intensified daily activity. It shared its extra revenue. It would be like asking other commercial companies, such as an engineering firm, or a textile concern producing fabric for uniforms – products essential for the nation – to share their profits with their rivals.

* * *

In addition to financial penalty, loss of 'repeat' traffic in the form of season ticketing, and the draining away of staff expertise, the railways were unable to sustain the good repair standards of their own equipment to the level of pre-war years. Not only was there 'dilution' of craftsmanship in the companies' works, there was a serious shortage of metal. The usual solution of sourcing metal – scrapping existing rolling stock – was not always available when even modern locomotives were awaiting repair, requiring older engines to continue working if they were unaffected.

In May 1918, Lloyd George's Cabinet was informed that no fewer than 4,000 locomotives were out of action, some 20 per cent of the national stock, the relevant minister (Churchill at that time) accepting that there had to be some relaxation of the strict steel quotas served on the railways. This backlog was building up as the railways were in the process of lending one locomotive in every fifteen to overseas war theatres. Even as late as September 1919, the Great Central had exactly 200 engines undergoing or awaiting repair (one-sixth of its operative strength of 1,252 locomotives), and had to borrow eighty-two goods engines either returned from the Continent or recently completed by commercial builders. Ironically, the locomotives were the GCR's own design of ROD 2-8-0.

In June 1917, REC Circular 1011 had intimated to the companies that there would be a relaxation in the strictly measured supply of steel to locomotive builders, and the railways were asked to specify what orders they would wish to place (through REC), in what quantity and class description, and in the case of a new design, with diagrams accompanying any application. But as if to balance this largesse, the REC had to inform the companies in that same summer that the Ministry of Munitions could not share sources of copper, a metal integral to armaments' production, unless it was required for firebox repairs and where no substitute material was available. In any event, the relaxation of steel supply for locomotive repairs was for commercial builders, and did not address the companies' own shortage of steel, from Eastleigh (Walker's own company's Works) to Lochgorm at Inverness.

There is evidence of a number of new locomotive classes being ordered from commercial builders by companies perfectly capable of delivering their own designs, and while this was not unusual, there is certainly little sign of railways 'growing their own'. That would mean returning engineering workshops back to their original constructional function for what might prove to be a short production line of engines, at a time when the military was queuing up with orders. Nevertheless, historian David Stevenson, who has carried out primary research on the subject of locomotive renewals, believes that the railways carried on to the end of 1918 with more resilience shown by those in either the USA or Canada.

The Sacrifice

This had been a war where, in the words of Siegfried Sassoon, 'drafts of volunteers were now droves of victims'. It would be invidious to suggest that railways were victims too, but they certainly were not victors.

No one would say that any one of the companies found more of its employees making the supreme sacrifice in comparison to any other. There would seem to be no reason why this would be so, but some casualty lists were longer than others. There is anecdotal evidence that recruiting staff were instructed to immediately allocate railwaymen to the Royal Engineers, but this might have been countermanded as the scale of railway staff enlistment became clear, or, perhaps more likely, the need for more infantry became pressing as the war went on. We have already seen that the ROD was encountering difficulties in recruiting even 'B' class soldiers to its ranks in 1917, and there is some evidence (hopefully fictional) that a doctor would 'pass' an entire roomful of soldiers as fit for combat without troubling to examine any of them. In any event, ex-railwaymen such as the aforementioned Norman McKillop found themselves serving in or alongside infantry.

According to the (regrettably brief) details recorded by Edwin Pratt in his *British Railways in the Great War*, the Midland suffered by far the largest number of casualties, some 6,451. This would of course include the 'missing', but also soldiers wounded, presumably seriously enough to prevent a return to employment. With the company having lost 21,813 men to the forces, almost 30 per cent of its staff complement, the casualty rate was horrendous – nearly one in three. (The company's memorial in Derby, unveiled in December 1921 and recently rededicated, gives the actual death toll as 2,833: Pratt's figure included missing and seriously wounded.) The Great Central's list is even worse, although from a smaller enlistment total. The London & North Western suffered 3,719 casualties out of the 31,742 that enlisted, representing more than one-third of the entire staff. The North Eastern accounted more than 2,100 dead or seriously wounded out of the 18,339 who enlisted, compared to the Great Western's 2,129 out of 25,479 (just 9 per cent). Effectively, the NER's casualty list was nearly 50 per cent more than Swindon's in this lottery of death or wounding.

Heaviest Casualty Rates for Britain's Railway Staff in WW1.
(Arranged by per cent of those enlisting. 1921 figures.)

Company	Enlisted	% of employed	Casualties	% of enlisted
Great Central	10,190	30	3,686	36.1
Midland	21,813	29	6,451	29.5
LNW	31,742	34	3,719	11.7
North Eastern	18,339	34	2,100*	11.4
South Eastern	5,074	24	499*	9.8
Great Northern	10,038	30	980*	9.7
Great Western	25,479	32	2,219*	8.7

*Pratt lists these as fatalities, rather than casualties, possibly concealing even worse overall figures. No comparative figures were rendered for the Great Eastern (9,734 enlisted), Lancashire & Yorkshire, London & South Western, and some smaller companies. GCR data is from Dow (qv). NER later commemorated 2,236 dead, not 'casualties'.

Casualty figures included wounded in most cases above, and at least one company, the North Western, addressed the need for prosthetics. Its company history, published in 1920, boasted thirty-five years' experience in manufacturing artificial limbs in its joinery shop at Crewe for the use of the company's own employees crippled as a result of accidents sustained in the performance of their duties … models of the most approved design [of prosthetic limbs] were being demonstrated to the War Office, and subsequently adopted for the use and benefit of men crippled in the service of their country.

* * *

In a sermon preached at the St Paul's memorial service for fallen railwaymen in May 1919, the Bishop of Peterborough pointed out that 'railwaymen had, at their country's call, come forward from workshop, from footplate, from signal box, from platform, from manager's office, and from platelayer's cabin'. This was obviously meant as a compliment to the patriotic spirit shown by those employed on Britain's railways, but could also be seen as an uncontrolled draining of qualified, experienced staff from one the nation's most important commercial concerns. And the episcopal pronouncement was contrary to that made by Sir Herbert Walker in REC Circular 61, when he declared that a railwayman 'is rendering as good service to the State by remaining at his employment as he could possibly be if he enlisted with the Forces'.

Walker's comment is commensurate with the view – and the Continental view – of a railway as a vital adjunct of the state, and of its war machine. If Walker's instructions had been followed properly – and they were unfortunately late in being issued – the railways would have been able to offer the best possible service to the military without taking on inexperienced workers, whether youths or women. Admittedly, it was probably impossible to stop men from volunteering as they were only too happy to leave behind poorly paid, menial labour, but from early 1915, when Kitchener began to eye up the railway companies as manpower 'banks', a stronger defence could have been made by railway managers who were coming under increasing pressure of military traffic demands. This might, just might, have convinced the Army commanders, denied 184,000 soldiers – three times the size of the Army thought large enough to repulse the Germans in August 1914 – that their method of waging war, of pitching a seemingly endless supply of men into the mincing machine of the Western Front, was illogical, wasteful, and downright immoral.

It remains to be added that Britain's railwaymen among them won no fewer than 5,357 decorations, including six Victoria Crosses, 283 Military Crosses (officers only), 2,517 Military Medals (other ranks), and 649 Mentions in Despatches. At least one company director is known to have given his life to the cause: the NER's Earl of Feversham, killed at the Somme in September 1916.

This was a nation, which, unlike France, Germany, and Russia, did not own or manage a single mile of railway, a nation where these vital sinews of communication were in the hands of those simply making profits for themselves. The consequences of this were low wages, awful working conditions, and poor or non-existent pension arrangements for their workers. So railwaymen were only too eager to 'come forward' from linesides, footplates, platelayers' cabins etc, for an occupation promising excitement, public acclamation, and foreign travel.

* * *

A number of memorial services followed the ending of the war, mostly around the time that the armistice of 11 November 1918 was effectively confirmed six months later. The largest of these was at London's St Paul's Cathedral, on 14 May 1919, attended by King George V, Queen Alexandra, and Princess Victoria. 3,000 members of bereaved families were present, with music provided by an orchestra drawn on a number of railway company staffs, including women. This was believed to be the first time that women had taken part in a service 'in the history of the edifice' of St Paul's, as Edwin Pratt records. Conducted by Colonel Galloway, a GER director, the orchestra and congregation opened with 'Onward Christian Soldiers' before listening to a sermon from the Bishop of Peterborough (quoted above), who clearly saw the nation's prime transport network as nothing more than a manpower reservoir.

The royal party finally left the cathedral to the strains of Handel's 'Hallelujah Chorus', and the monarch later commented on how pleased he was to see women taking part in the service. It should be noted that all this was for railwaymen who had paid with their lives, or even just their health, by enlisting, not for any other 'sacrifices' caused by inexperienced staff working in conditions made more than usually dangerous by lighting restrictions, bombing, or bombardment.

Beyond London, memorial services took place in many cathedrals and churches in England and Wales at this time. The Midland Railway organised services for its enlisted casualties (the greatest number of any company), at Derby, Nottingham, and Sheffield, while the North Eastern called ceremonies at Newcastle-upon-Tyne, York, and Hull. Municipal services were held at cathedrals in Manchester, Carlisle, Bristol, Llandaff, Bangor, and Birmingham, and there were additional ceremonies at two churches in London and one in Cardiff.

Following commemorative services, it was decided to produce permanent memorials to the fallen, ironically at a time when the companies themselves were about to become part of history. Where granite was being used for a memorial, company boards were warned that it would be advisable to discuss alternative quarry sources with commissioned artists, as so many memorials were planned from 1920 onwards, with even villages creating their own, that demand was beginning to outstrip supply. Metal memorials, archways, and gates were also designed for commemoration purposes.

Locomotives might have been looked on as potential mobile monuments, but were fewer in number than might have been expected. The most impressive of these was probably the Great Central's graceful 4-6-0 named *Valour*, with a dedication to the company's war dead on a nameplate on the locomotive's 'paddle box'. On the other hand, the cheapest-looking was Ole Bill a North British class C 0-6-0 whose name was simply painted on the central splasher. This was one of twenty-five NBR engines named after French and British commanders and battles in the Great War; this particular locomotive commemorating Bruce Bairnsfather's cartoon character, a humble soldier who had been 'out since Mons'. Since the engine had actually served in France, the apparent parsimony of its naming can surely be forgiven. It served its later owners, the LNER, for another twenty years, until 1939.

In 1927, the LMSR took delivery of the 'Royal Scot' 4-6-0s for express work, and the class was partially, and later wholly, named after units of the armed services. One of these was named 'Old Contemptibles', a title which baffled this author when, as a young railway enthusiast, I first saw this engine. As rebuilt by Stanier from 1943 onwards, this class was ranked among the most handsome steam locomotives operated by British Railways, and their naming was demonstrably a way of ensuring a memorable tribute to the 'little army' so dismissed by the Kaiser, but also to the huge host which Britain later placed in the field.

***

In total, some forty-five memorials to railwaymen were established in or near Britain's railway stations. The LB&SCR created three, two in London and one in Brighton, the Midland, and GNR (I) two each. The North Western resolved to have a chain of local memorials to commemorate men from individual districts – Birmingham (New Street) had two, one of which still survives, while the other has been moved to the National Memorial Arboretum. It was this company which erected what is perhaps the most impressive monument in the shape of the obelisk outside Euston, although the South Western's Victory Arch at Waterloo is equally admirable. The Midland, the company with the worst casualty list, chose its home city of Derby for the erection of a cenotaph designed by Edwin Lutyens, a busy artist also responsible for the needle-like obelisk commemorating the NER's dead just next to the city walls at York.

A company memorial which attracted a history of its own was the Great Eastern's at Liverpool Street. Consisting of marble tablets set into a wall, it was unveiled by General Sir Henry Wilson on 22 June 1922, only for Wilson to return home that day to find an IRA assassin awaiting him. A side panel now commemorates this atrocity which 'occurred within two hours of his unveiling of the adjoining memorial'. A memorial to Captain Fryatt is also there (see the chapter on railways' maritime services).

Curiously, only one memorial received a royal unveiling in the immediate post-war years – the South Western's archway at Waterloo, which Queen Mary 'opened' on 21 March 1922. It would survive being damaged by a German bomb in the next war. Field Marshal (soon to be Earl) Haig carried out unveilings at five locations – for the Great Northern, North Western, Great Central, Lancashire & Yorkshire, and G&SWR. All memorials were completed before the companies lost their identities in the Grouping of 1923, with the exception of the North Eastern's at York, and the Hull & Barnsley's in Hull (in fact the latter company had been absorbed by the North Eastern before the Grouping). The North Eastern's railways were slower to make this commemoration than elsewhere, in 1924, as Lutyens's original design for the York memorial would have intruded on the city's ancient walls, and had to be modified. The H & B's memorial was privately financed. These measured acts of remembrance were in pointed contrast to the alacrity with which NER staff threw themselves into the conflict, starting with Mons in 1914.

Conclusion

One of Douglas Haig's biographers has made the point that, whatever you might think of him, the senior British commander on the Western Front for three years, he at least *won*. It could equally be said that he was on the side which managed not to lose. If modern historians take the view that Germany was as much a land-grabbing aggressor in 1914 as in 1940, then the First World War had to be fought, and was not by any means an unnecessary conflict, a competitive clash of rival capitalist trading blocs. Britain was responding to the breach of the 1839 treaty which guaranteed Belgium's security, but there was also a motive of self-preservation in not allowing the nearest part of the Continental coast to fall into the hands of an aggressive power. Whatever Francophobes may say, no one in England ever sleeps badly because Boulogne or Dunkirk are in the hands of the French.

But whether war was necessary, and no matter how badly it was conducted on the battlefield, Britain's railways made a corporate contribution, which, in terms of effort and valour, was unequalled by any other civilian organisation, except the Merchant Marine (and that also included railwaymen). Yet, by closing branch lines and wayside stations from 1917, in sending track parts and vehicles abroad, the railways adopted a passive, defeatist profile in the UK – opening the way for motor vehicles operated under untrammelled trading conditions.

If the railways' support was essential – as Haig clearly thought it was – surely a price could have been exacted from Government which would have guaranteed the railways' primary place in Britain's transport industry? The 1919 Act establishing the new Transport Ministry would have been an ideal opportunity to do so, even if it meant introducing a measure of control on future transport, particularly in relation to the use of road vehicles by commercial firms. Perhaps this would have required a crystal ball for use in railway boardrooms, but the free trading conditions for commercial road users would begin as soon as the demobilisation programmes were under way, and surplus vehicles became cheaply available. Meanwhile, railways were seeing their running costs rising by more than 60 per cent, and that fails to take into account the reduction in working hours, and the new operating practices that would necessitate. Yet, the railwaymen deserved more pay and better conditions, just as railways merited a more sympathetic attitude from Westminster and Whitehall.

* * *

In fairness to the railway managers making up the REC, it should be said that they succeeded in tightening up their organisation as the war went on. Although there was a curious change of policy as early as September 1914, when individual brigade headquarters were encouraged to make transport arrangements with their 'nearest' railway company, this new system lasted barely a year. It could hardly have been superior to the earliest links between commands and their 'Secretary' companies which had served the BEF so well, and helped change the course of the war at the Marne. By the end of hostilities, the magazine *Engineering* paid the following compliment: 'Sir Herbert Walker and his colleagues on the REC have been too modest, [and] the public do not know what they have achieved.' At the outbreak of the next war in 1939, a new Minister of Transport (Reith) was told that 'the railways run themselves through the REC', and a recent historian, Ian Beckett, has pointed out that the railway network 'was pointedly administered not by the government but for the government'. Edwin Pratt believed that the word 'control' in official documents was misleading and that the government of the day was merely looking to 'command the railway resources of the country'.

But this all started with a muddled declaration of war, and when one reads of historians debating when exactly the First World War broke out, it seems to be ignored that many railways had already made preparatory arrangements to handle huge movements of troops. Meanwhile, the Royal Navy was taking up railway ships while its political head, the First Lord of the Admiralty, was playing with his children on Cromer beach, fully ten days before Prime Minister Asquith decided, after much hesitation, to present Germany with an ultimatum. Thus had begun the war to end all wars.

* * *

Looking back from the 1970s, Alan Clark wrote in his book *The Donkeys* that the British officer class in the First World War had commanded 'the greatest army that the Empire had ever put in the field in the past, or was ever to amass in the future … twice in two successive years [it was] ravaged in hopeless offensives, who were in a single day to lose more men than in any other army in the history of the world'.

It was for all this that Britain's railways carried and ferried troops to the battlefield, supplied ambulance trains to bring so many of them back, took civilians to and from work, and, surprisingly, to and from their holidays. Coal was carried in unprecedented amounts and over unforeseen distances, while new vehicles were devised for the transport of tanks and guns. Explosives were carried daily in quantities previously unimaginable from munition factories the size of cities, built with materials ferried in by train. Air raids were endured by staff already shorthanded, railwaymen were killed by enemy shelling, and railway-owned ships were sailed through seas made many times more hostile, by mine and submarine, than ever before. Railway factories and repair shops produced hardware for the forces while their own rolling stock succumbed to near-neglect. One historian, C. Hamilton Ellis, estimates that Britain's railways rendered services worth £126,192,000 to the Government during the war, the equivalent of around £10 billion in modern terms, but so much of this dedication was unquantifiable.

The railways did everything for the Army and, with huge numbers of railwaymen enlisting, even did much of the fighting for it. But within five years, railway owners were anxious to seek financial security through the Grouping. Within ten years, railways found themselves unable to reach Government-set targets, unrealistically based on figures for 1913.

Railways had defeat in view, even in their hour of victory.

Abbreviations

ARLE	Association of Railway Locomotive Engineers
ASLEF	Associated Society of Locomotive Engineers and Firemen
BEF	British Expeditionary Force
Bn	Battalion
CME	Chief Mechanical Engineer
C&W	Carriage and Wagon (Works)
DORA	Defence of the Realm Acts
ECML	East Coast Main Line
GM	General Manager
GCR	Great Central Railway
GER	Great Eastern Railway
GNR	Great Northern Railway
GWR	Great Western Railway
L&Y	Lancashire & Yorkshire Railway
L&NWR	London & North Western Railway
L&SWR	London & South Western Railway
NUR	National Union of Railwaymen
RAMC	Royal Army Medical Corps
REC	Railway Executive Committee
ROF	Royal Ordnance Factory
SECR	South Eastern & Chatham Railway
WCML	West Coast Main Line

Acknowledgements

The author has carried out primary research in the archival papers of the Railway Executive Committee (BR/REC/S/A1/1, 22, and 23, NAS), principally Circulars 4, 61, 102, 120, 141, 215, 315, 330, 375, 384, 490, 563, 572, 573, 580, 589, 611, 622, 632, 647, 748, 913, 941, 1010 and 1011. Also, in a number of railway companies' files.

Acknowledgement must be given to the historical volumes of the journalist for *The Times*, Edwin Pratt. Pratt's *British Railways and the Great War* was one of the last books he wrote, and was based on interviews with railway company officials. It is a formidable piece of historical reporting, although women's historian Helena Wojtczak is critical of Pratt's handling of the female contribution to railway operations.

This author acknowledges research assistance kindly provided by Richard Lacey and Marilyn Mullay, although all conclusions and opinions are the author's own. The staff at the National Archives of Scotland, National Library, and Edinburgh City Libraries are thanked for their usual high standard of service.

Bibliography

Railway Titles

Darroch, G. R. S., *Deeds of a Great Railway* [L&NWR] (John Murray, 1920).

Dow, G., *Great Central Vol. 3* (Ian Allan, 1965).

Ellis, C. H., *British Railway History, 1877–1947*, 2 (Allen & Unwin, 1959).

Gould, D., *The South-Eastern & Chatham Railway in the 1914–18 War* (Oakwood, 1981).

Hamilton, J. A. B., *Britain's Railways in the First World War* (Allen & Unwin, 1967).

Helm, J. W. E., 'The Bombing of Britain's Railways: A War Diary, 1914–1918', *Backtrack*, 20 (2006).

Hunter, D. L. G., *The Highland Railway in Retrospect* (Moorfoot, 1988).

McKillop, N., *Enginemen Elite* (Ian Allan, 1958).

Mullay, A. J., 'Britain's Railway Canals', *Railway Archive*, 30–32 (2010/11).

Mullay, A. J., *For the King's Service: Railway Ships at War* (Pendragon, 2008).

Pratt, E. A., *British Railways and the Great War Vol. II* (Selwyn & Blount, 1921).

RCTS, *A Detailed History of BR Standard Steam Locomotives*, 1 (1994).

Railway Yearbooks (1914–20).

Scholey, K., 'Railway War Memorials', *Backtrack*, 10 pt 12 (1996).

Wojtczak, H., *Railwaywomen: Exploitation, Betrayal and Triumph* (Hastings Press, 2005).

Wolmar, C., *Engines of War: How Wars Were Won and Lost on the Railways* (Atlantic, 2012).

Military Titles

Anonymous [Sassoon, S.], *Memoirs of an Infantry Officer* (London: Faber & Faber, 1930).

Clark, A., *The Donkeys* (London, Hutchinson, 1961).

Doyle, P., and J. Walker, *Trench Talk: Words of the First World War* (Staplehurst: Spellmount, 2012).

Fay, S., *The War Office at War* (Wakefield: EP, 1973) [Facsimile of 1937 edition].

Gilbert, Sir Martin, *First World War* (London: HarperCollins, 1995).

Hastings, Sir Max, *Catastrophe: Europe Goes to War 1914* (London: Collins, 2013).

Horsfall, J., and N. Cave, *Battleground Europe. Mons 1914* (Barnsley: Leo Cooper, 2000).

Layman, R. D., *Before the Aircraft Carrier: the Development of Aviation Vessels, 1849–1922* (London, Conway Maritime, 1989).

Paxman, J., *Great Britain's Great War* (New York: Viking, 2013).

Reith, John (later Lord), *Wearing Spurs* (London: Hutchison, 1966).

Richards, F., *Old Soldiers Never Die* (Peterborough: Krijnen & Langley, 2004). [1933 edition annotated by the publishers].

Routledge, G. L., *Gretna's Secret War* (Carlisle: Bookcase, 1999).

Stevenson, D., *With Our Backs to the Wall: Victory and Defeat in 1918* (London: Allen Lane, 2011).

Strachan, H., *The First World War. To Arms*, 1 (Oxford: OUP, 2001).

Taylor, A. J. P., *War by Timetable: How the First World War Began* (London: Macdonald, 1969).

War Office, *Statistics of the Military Effort of the British Empire during the Great War* (London: HMSO, 1922).

Index